AF327994

JOE LOUIS

Rugio Vitale

MELROSE SQUARE PUBLISHING COMPANY
LOS ANGELES, CALIFORNIA

Editors Note: At several points in the early pages of this work, Joe Louis is referred to as "champ" before the actual feat was accomplished. The title, in these instances, is bestowed out of respect rather than ignorance, and none but the hardest of hearts would dare take that title away. Louis was always, and will always remain, a champion.

MELROSE SQUARE BLACK AMERICAN SERIES

ELLA FITZGERALD
singer

NAT TURNER
slave revolt leader

PAUL ROBESON
singer and actor

JACKIE ROBINSON
baseball great

LOUIS ARMSTRONG
musician

SCOTT JOPLIN
composer

MATTHEW HENSON
explorer

MALCOLM X
militant black leader

CHESTER HIMES
author

SOJOURNER TRUTH
antislavery activist

BILLIE HOLIDAY
singer

RICHARD WRIGHT
writer

ALTHEA GIBSON
tennis champion

JAMES BALDWIN
author

JESSE OWENS
olympics star

MARCUS GARVEY
black nationalist leader

JOE
LOUIS

June 18, 1941: Billy Conn slipped and fell in the first round of his fight with heavyweight champion Joe Louis at the New York City Polo Grounds. Louis won by a knockout.

1

It was 1936, and "jolting" Joe Louis, the Brown Bomber, the black man who was to become a legend in his own time, stood meekly before President Franklin D. Roosevelt in the White House, Washington, D.C. Earlier that same year, Joe had been invited to attend the Negro Elks convention in Washington where he was awared an honorary life-membership gold card in the Elks and rode in the marshal's car in the organization's parade. Now, standing before FDR, brought to the White House in a presidential limousine, the man who was to make boxing history, the man whose name would eventually become a household word—as popular as the "breakfast of champions"—was being asked, but subtly, of course, always subtly in politics, to defend the

United States against the scourge of Nazism.

After greeting Louis warmly, FDR said, "Lean over, Joe, so I can feel your muscles."

Louis complied.

FDR nodded in appreciation. "Joe, we need muscles like yours to beat Germany."

Purportedly, that was all Roosevelt said. But later, when the story got out and repeated, it came out that the President had said something like, "Joe, beat Schmeling to prove to the world that we can beat Germany."

Always a simple man, lacking the education, Louis found himself smack in the middle of the world's political arena. In Europe, the Nazis were preparing to goose-step their way across continents, crushing whatever lay in their path. Antisemetisim was already rearing its ugly swastika head. Nor did Hitler's white supremacy philosophy leave room for black people, and Schmeling, the Aryan hope, the German who had beaten Louis before—thereby supposedly proving Hitler's theory in the boxing ring—loomed arrogant in the land of the coming Storm Trooper, haloed even more arrogantly by Japan's rising sun.

"People put it out that I hated Schmeling for hitting me after the bell in that first fight," Louis once clarified for newsmen. "I never hated him. We became friends. After the fight, he sent me one of those German cuckoo clocks. Ain't no reason to hate a man just because he beats you in a fight."

Such is the simple man's philosophy. But there was hate involved, though not on Joe's part. Nazi hate. Hate for blacks. Friends, associates, even casual acquaintances, all have characterized Louis as a man whose good will and boxing talent left no room for this type of emotion. Yet the press, the politics involved—

black vs. white, the Aryan dogmas opposing the American way—built the second Louis-Schmeling fight into a battle of philosophies. Simple man that he was, the Brown Bomber was to enter the ring in Yankee Stadium on June 28, 1938 as a hard-fisted promise to the threat Adolph Hitler was preparing to issue to the world at large and the United States in particular. No one but a champ could have stepped into that ring without hate.

There were more than 42,000 spectators cramming the seats in Yankee Stadium when Louis climbed through the ropes, a fantastic 10-to-1 favorite in his first fight with Schmeling. The fight had been scheduled for the night before. It rained, perhaps an ominous sign. Schmeling sat in his corner, black hair neatly combed and face inscrutable. His concentration was unaffected by the noisy spectators, the thick air of excitement and barely hidden blood lust that accompanies all championship prizefights. "Schmeling, he a cool man," Louis admits to having thought when he saw the German sitting across the ring from him that night.

The *clang-clang* of the bell at ringside silenced the crowd. All eyes were on the opponents as they approached center-stage in the roped-in arena. The German's left arm was extended, right fist cocked at his chest and chin tucked in at his collarbone. He was ready for the Bomber, knew Joe's style. It was not going to be the laydown the oddsmakers had predicted.

For three tense rounds, Louis could not land the solid right that had put so many of his previous opponents away. Instead, he depended almost totally on his left. A jab opened a cut under Schmeling's right eye. The crowd roared. But the German ignored the trickle of blood, and Louis, striking out again and again with the left, was confronted by the same obstinacy, the same push, that drove hundreds of thousands of German soldiers across the impossible wastelands of Siberia. Was Hitler right after all? Was the Nazi war and human fighting machine really omnipotent?

It happened in the fourth round. Louis shifted to throw a left jab, and *zap!* Schmeling countered: he crossed Joe's left with a right that caught the champ on the chin. Another slamming right followed, jolting Joe's jaw. The champ sank to the canvas. Never before in his professional career had Louis been down. The crowd stood awe struck as Joe heard the referee count. The count reached three. Joe sprang up, shook off the worst of the blows and finished the round.

In his corner, Blackburn, Louis' trainer since his first year as a pro, scolded him loudly. "I *told* you to watch out for that *right*," Blackburn screamed over the roar of the stadium crowd. Joe was still fuzzy, still shaking loose from the surprise blows hammered home by Schmeling. Indeed, Blackburn had warned him time and again. Blackburn, if not Joe, knew that Schmeling had done his homework exceptionally well. In a recent fight between Louis and Paolino Uzcudun, a bulky Basque, the German was purportedly in the waning days of his boxing career. But he had always been a thoughtful student of the sport and the opportunity to watch Louis in action against Uzcudun was a laboratory session. "I seez somezing," Schmeling told reporters afterward. And now, in Yankee Stadium, the lights blaring hotly overhead and the crowd at the edge of their seats because jolting-Joe had gone down for a three-count, whatever it was Schmeling saw, whatever flaw in Joe's style, was about to be put to the ultimate test. The German maintained his composure.

In the fifth round, Schmeling's right fist was back in Joe's bruised face . . . another hard right to the jaw.

Louis' ears rang. His already swollen jaw felt heavy and painful. He heard the bell announcing the end of the round and dropped his guard. His hands were heavy, arms leaden. Another hard right crashed into his face— the controversial blow *after* the bell that Louis has never held animosity for—sent him sprawling to the canvas for the second time in his professional career. Louis' handlers rushed in and pulled him into his corner. Referee Donovan warned Schmeling against hitting after the bell.

Was the punch after the bell intentional? The Nazi way? Joe thinks not . . . such would be unsportsman like, and there is a *code* in the ring. Intentional or not, most experts agree that this was the punch that decided the fight. Louis, already hurting from the third round knockdown, was a mere caricature of himself when he answered the bell for the sixth. He was badly beaten. Schmeling did not finish him off until the twelfth round, but it seemed, after the blow that came *after* the bell, that the end was a foregone conclusion, no matter how courageously Joe tried to regain what was lost in the two knockdowns.

The final punch was another hard right to the jaw. Louis went down slowly, a wounded Goliath. Stretching out on the unfamiliar, dirty canvas, the stadium crowd on their feet and screaming for the Brown Bomber to rise, Joe rested his head on his right glove. "When the referee counted," he admitted later, "it came to me faint, like a whisper. It didn't make no difference."

It was the first defeat suffered by the Brown Bomber in 28 professional fights. The press, his fans, the world—with the exception of Germany- had built him up to be a superman, and he had been proved vulnerable. Worse, by a German! Schmeling, the Aryan hope, had indeed seen "somezing" during the Louis Uzcudun fight. It had to do with Louis' habit of dropping his left arm after throwing a jab, thereby exposing himself to the German's deadly right cross. Whether it was the blow landed after the bell ending the fifth, what happened prior or subsequent to it, Max Schmeling's keen eye and quick reflex had taken deadly advantage of the champion's flaw. An astounded spectator crowd left Yankee Stadium that night. But no one was more astounded than the Brown Bomber himself.

Alfred Hitchcock could not have added more intrigue, and there was even more racist politics—in the press, over the international airways—between Joe's first and second fight with Max Schmeling. In Detroit, recuperating not so much from the physical but from the *psychological* affects of the bout, Joe tried to remember how it had been in the last minutes and hours after the knockout by Schmeling. Blackburn—good old Blackburn—had to apply ice packs to Joe's eyes and cheeks. Back at the Theresa, the hotel in Harlem where he and his entourage stayed, Joe had looked dolefully into the mirror and shuddered. "Your head looks like a watermelon," Vunice, his sister, had commented. But nobody laughed, not even a little. Nobody thought it was even remotely funny. Nobody had ever seen jolting-Joe defeated before.

The swelling was gone within a few days but the cold fact of defeat lingered. With Marva, his wife, Joe left New York for his mother's place in Detroit. Momma treated her son—hulking though he was—as a youngster again, cooking his favorite boyhood meals, offering homespun philosophy and words of consolation, almost as if he had been in a street fight with one of the bad kids from the neighborhood and had come home crying. Joe's spirit nourished. Before long, he was moving about town, seeing old friends and such, his old self again. He was barely twenty two after all. And one knockout, however devastating to one's pride, did not a has-been prizefighter make.

The pain of personal defeat was reignited by over-zealous newsmen. Had Joe Louis, a national black hero, let his people down by losing to Schmeling? Had he set race relations back in America, unwittingly added another cudgel to the Hitler-minded hands guiding the U.S. Nazi Bund? Joe was no sociologist—a simple man—but he sensed that victory or defeat in the boxing ring would not diminish or increase racism in America. "When I lost to Schmeling," he told one obnoxious newsman, "I didn't hurt my people. There are just as many Negro doctors, lawyers and politicians as before I was whupped. And none of the poor ain't suddenly rich either."

The German propaganda machine felt otherwise. Nazi newsmen made much of the defeat of a Negro, an *American* Negro, by a member of the superior German race. And they would make even more of the Louis defeat before the wounded Goliath stepped through the ropes to face Max Schmeling a second time.

In Detroit, Joe played golf regularly. Golf became his favorite pastime. Marva, his wife, once complained publicly that "golf seemed to be the most important thing in Joe's life . . . more important than women." Joe rode horses and took in shows to while away the time. He attempted to enjoy himself away from boxing. He tried some of this, some of that, but at the back of his mind was a nagging compulsion to prove to himself and to the world that the knockout by Schmeling had not finished him as a prizefighter. He tried a variety of activities, other ways to forget. Nothing he did in the way of recreation—not even his cherished golf—seemed to please him for long, and the prodding via the news media continued. The waiting finally ended when a match between Joe and Jack Sharkey was arranged for Yankee Stadium. Sharkey had beaten Schmeling for the championship four years earlier and then lost to Primo Carnera, but still ranked as one of the top contenders. Sharkey was "making a comeback," the media contended. The promoter for the fight, Mike Jacobs, a shrewd businessman who was destined to keep his finger in the Joe Louis pie, played Sharkey up as the *perfect opponent* for Louis' reentry into the area where Schmeling had put him down for the count.

Louis had trained in Lakewood for the Schmeling bout. It was there that he was introduced to golf, and there, too, that he broke training, ignoring Blackburn's entreaties, playing the green almost daily with some of the newsmen assigned to cover the camp's activities. Chappie, that golf ain't good for you," Blackburn had warned the champ over and over again. It's okay," Louis had countered. "I walk. That's good training for my legs."

"The timing's different," Blackburn tried to explain. "Them muscles you use in golf, they ain't the same ones you use hitting a man. Besides, being out in the sun don't do you no good. You'll be dried out time the fight comes around."

But the folly of all that was behind him now. In the training ring, in Lakewood before the first Schmeling fight, Joe had proceeded to knock down his sparring partners and apprehension had waned somewhat. But the truth in Blackburn's warnings had come across dramatically in the outcome of that first fight. Now, training for Sharkey, Joe was somewhat the wiser for wear. The Louis entourage returned to Pompton Lakes, New Jersey—training grounds before the Schmeling fight—to prepare for the champ's reentry.

Back at the old training grounds in Pompton Lakes, newsmen approached Joe with a different strategy. "Did the defeat by Schmeling take the heart out of you, Joe?"

Louis' responses committed him to atoning for the Schmeling defeat. Blackburn listened, gritted his teeth and worked Joe harder than he had ever worked him before. He stressed defense against the right hand punch that had proved itself deadly in the Schmeling bout. He ordered Louis' sparring partners to throw the right as hard and as often as they could . . . "try to *hit 'im!* That's what Sharkey's gonna try," Blackburn said. "Lead to that man, and he'll try to hit you with rights, the way Schmeling did. Watch for it, Joe. Watch all the time for it."

Joe followed Blackburn's instructions to the letter throughout training. On the night of the Sharkey fight, the lights in Yankee Stadium blaring hot overhead again, the Brown Bomber came out of his corner with the memory of Schmeling's right hand blows foremost in his mind. It would not happen again, he had promised newsmen, trainer and Marva alike. The latter, against her better judgment, had been persuaded by a woman reporter to attend the Schmeling fight. She had wanted to flee when Joe was knocked down the first time, not wanting to see more. But her companion insisted she stay. And for too many nights after that first Schmeling fight she had experienced nightmares. She would see her husband with his face swollen and eyes closed, Schmeling's right hand landing again and again. Joe, too, had experienced such nightmares. His were waking dreams that began when he looked into the mirror at the Hotel Theresa in Harlem, and heard Vunice, his sister, say that his face was a "watermelon-like" thing. Joe was determined, in the ring now with

Jack Sharkey, that such nightmares—waking or otherwise—would never recur.

Following Blackburn's instructions as he had done throughout training, Louis jabbed away at Sharkey's head through the first round. Sharkey moved inside the jab and threw a hard right, a bad copy of Schmeling's approach, but using the same strategy. Louis blocked the attempt. Then, responding with a right of his own, Joe hurt Sharkey badly just before the end of the first round.

It took the Brown Bomber two more rounds to finish the would-be contender. The final, crushing punch was another right to the jaw, the crowd on its feet and roaring for a different reason this time. Jack Sharkey wavering . . . falling . . . on the canvas, flat on his face. The old Joe Louis, the destructive one, the one who had entered the ring a 10-to-1 favorite in the first Schmeling fight was back, and for keeps.

In the Louis dressing room after the fight, Blackburn told newsmen, "Joe's mad at Schmeling, but Sharkey, he paid for it."

Approximately one month after the Sharkey fight, Louis was back in the ring, this time in Philadelphia. In that fight, he flattened Al Ettore in five rounds. Seventeen days later, barely time to catch his breath for the average fighter, Joe fought Jorge Brescia, an Argentine, at the Hippodrome in New York. The bout lasted only three rounds, another knockout by Louis. The tight schedule had been purposefully arranged to keep Joe's mind on boxing and put the Brown Bomber back in the public eye. Now, once again, he was "the greatest," long before Cassius Clay. He went on an exhibition tour, knocking out four more opponents in South Bend and New Orleans. In Cleveland, a fight slated for ten rounds, he disposed of Eddie Simms in the first. He hit Simms so hard that the boxer stared groggily up at referee Arthur Donovan, and said, "Let's go on the roof. I want to get some fresh air."

Joe needed to get back whatever it was he had lost in the first Schmeling fight. But "saying" was easier than "doing." Schmeling seemed content to rest on his laurels, and there were other contenders for the heavyweight crown.

Early in 1937, Louis fought Bob Pastor in Madison Square Garden. Bookmakers picked Joe as a 2-to-1 favorite to score a knockout, but wily Jim Johnston had not been considered in their calculations. Now the boxing intrigue thickened; Johnston, fight promoter for the Garden and therefore ineligible to manage a prizefighter, nonetheless handled Pastor's affairs. Johnston had never forgotten that he was turned down cold when he offered his services—for the standard percentage—as exclusive promoter for Louis. Now he mapped Pastor's strategy. He ordered his fighter to keep on the move throughout the fight. "Louis can't hit what don't stand still," he proclaimed.

Pastor ran for ten rounds, avoiding the knockout punch that was again becoming Louis' claim to boxing fame and the thing designed to get him a rematch with Schmeling. "Pin him in the corner," Blackburn pleaded with Joe from outside the ring.

But Pastor remained elusive, it not aggresive. When the bout was over, a decision, Louis' hand was again raised in victory. He had won it hands down. But wily Jim Johnston had also won: no knockout, another mar on the Brown Bomber's track record.

"I felt bad about the fight," Louis remembers. Johnston gloated. The rematch with Schmeling, partially because of the Pastor bout, seemed to be slipping further and further away. Less than one month after the Pastor fight, Joe fought Natie Brown in Kansas City. It was like being mad at Schmeling and whipping Jack Sharkey all over again. Brown, by going the distance years before, had spoiled Joe's "coming out" party in Detroit on the night the New York sportswriters watched Brown Bomber in action for the first time. Louis had failed to put Brown's lights out that first time. This time Brown was knocked out in the fourth round.

Mike Jacobs and the 20th Century Sporting Club had been granted, over Johnston's request, exclusive promotional rights to Louis. Now *Jacobs* became the arch plotter in the far-reaching sports intrigue. Aware that Braddock, official heavyweight champion of the world, was under exclusive contract to Madison Square Garden, Jacobs set in motion a plot designed to deprive the Garden of Braddock's services for the title fight with Schmeling, scheduled for June 3, 1937 at the Madison Square Garden Bowl in Long Island City. Jacobs had already tried unsuccessfully to persuade Schmeling to give Joe a rematch. Schmeling had refused; the Nazi propaganda machine was still making much of the knockout. Instead, Schmeling had signed to fight Braddock under the Garden's auspices, and had returned to Germany comforted by the notion that he would soon bring the world heavyweight championship home to the *Vaterland*. Adolph Hitler's vile philosophy of Aryan surperiority was by this time a national policy in Germany. Placed in the hands of Paul Joseph Goebbels, *der Fuehrer's* propaganda chief, Louis' knockout by Schmeling assumed the many heads of the dreaded Hydra. Goebbels proceeded to use Schmeling, particularly the victory over a black American, as proof positive of Nazi dogma. A dwarfish man with a cippled foot and a neurotic personality, but nonetheless agile of mind, Goebbels supplied the right words for Schmeling to speak to the news media.

"The black man will always be afraid of me," the German press quoted Schmeling as saying. "He is inferior."

Living, as he was, in Nazi German, Schmeling was in no position to deny the statement, if, indeed, he ever did choose to deny it. This and subsequent press releases cost him any sympathy he might have gained as a result of Jacobs' plot to deprive him of a shot at Braddock's coveted title. Louis, passive as usual, still a simple man, docilely taking what the press had to give but giving it back ten-fold inside the ring, brushed off the comments. He respected Schmeling as a prizefighter. Politics remained beyond his scope of comprehension, and Germany, the Nazi dogmas, further beyond that. There was a Nazi Bund right here in America, more than enough racism to contend with on the streets of Chicago, Detroit, New York and other major U.S. cities.

Joe Gould, Braddock's manager, was a small, sharp-nosed little man who had been an insignificant factor in the fight business until Braddock came along and made the surprise climb to the heavyweight throne. Conspiratorial by nature and inclination, Gould quickly involved himself in Jacobs' scheme. In exchange for ten percent of Jacobs' net profits from heavyweight championship fights for the next ten years, he signed a contract that called for Braddock to defend his title against the Brown Bomber in Chicago's Comiskey Park on June 22, 1937. Years later, the conniving Gould would sue Jacobs for his and Braddock's share of the agreed upon profits, but at the time of the scheduled Louis-Braddock fight he was the wily promoter's close associate.

Madison Square Garden brought suit in federal court to enjoin Braddock, insisting, in the press and the courtroom, that he was obligated to contract to defend his title only under the auspices of the Garden. Jacobs ignored the threat of suit; Sol Strauss, his hard-of-hearing lawyer, a Pickwickian type, had read the contract between Braddock and the Garden and had reached the legal conclusion that it was invalid in equity because it tied Braddock to the Garden without imposing any obligation on the sporting arena. In federal court in Newark, New Jersey, Judge Guy L. Fake ruled against the Garden. Schmeling continued to train rigorously for the fight with Braddock. The New York State Athletic Commission even went through the pretense of holding the weigh-in ceremony for the fight scheduled for June 3, 1937. However, Madison Square Garden Bowl remained in darkness that night. The Braddock-Schmeling match was thereafter referred to as the "phantom fight."

Louis, meanwhile, had begun preparations for the championship bout. He and his entourage went to Stevensville, Michigan to relax. "Building up energy," Blackburn explained. And then to Kenosha, Wisconsin and in-earnest training on the pleasant shore of Lake Michigan.

It was a genial camp. Joe lived in a large brick house and the breeze that wafted in off the lake made leisure hours and sleeping even more pleasant. Harry Lenny was the newest element on the relocated training scene. He was a veteran trainer, had been brought into camp to teach the Brown Bomber how to defend properly against right hand punches. Blackburn was not upset by what some may have taken as a usurpage of his exclusive position. "If it helps Chappie become champ, it's good," he said.

A rigid training schedule was set up and strictly adhered to. Louis ran ten miles each morning, sparring on alternate days. Up at 5:00 a.m., he would lead Blackburn, and Carl Nelson, a Chicago detective hired on as Joe's bodyguard, into the half-light of breaking day, both men trailing him in a car as he ran across the undulating countryside. Then back into camp to sleep until 10:00 a.m. and a breakfast of orange juice, prunes, lamp chops or liver. A healthy regimen for a champ. Joe was restless, hitting his sparring partner as hard and as often as he could. The training was good but the days seemed to pass by too slowly. Meat and fish and vegetales were consumed before the ice cream that ended the day, and he was in bed by 9:00 p.m. He was in camp on his twenty-third birthday, May 13, 1937. A cake was baked. Everyone wished Joe well. The champ felt gratified. He was happy, if restless, certain again of his ability and in top shape. He was anxious to fight the official heavyweight champion of the world.

Braddock? A factor, nothing more. There was only one man who had ever put Joe Louis down on the canvas in his professional career, and Braddock, the official title holder, was merely a stepping stone to the German.

Louis, wearing his lucky blue bathrobe with red trim, was unruffled when he stepped through the ropes at Comiskey Park. He was not yet the king of the heavyweights. But his bearing, so regal, depicted great things to come. All that was left for the Brown Bomber to reach the coveted heights was for him to lay gloves on the enemy, in this case, Braddock.

"Chappie, this is it," Blackburn whispered to him over the noise of the crowd. "You come home champ tonight."

The bell rang before Joe could reply. Blackburn nodded. Joe moved away from his corner and toward Braddock, a man whose boxing style he knew inside out. Braddock, who had taken the title from Max Baer two years ago, had not engaged in a bout since. Surprising everyone with the outcome of the Baer fight, Braddock was labeled "Cinderella Man," coming, as he did, off the home relief rolls to achieve his greatest triumph. Now, in the ring with the younger, more agile Louis, Braddock appeared old, slow. He threw the first heavy punch of the fight, a hard right. Louis moved inside it, tried his jab.

The first left found Braddock's face. The crowd roared. Braddock countered with another right—more shouts from the spectators. Again the Brown Bomber stepped inside the righthand punch, this time responding with a sharp right of his own. Another right from Braddock and Louis was down.

Incredible! The noise from the crowd was a thunderclap that shook Comiskey Park. Was it happening again? Had the Brown Bomber found himself pitted against another Max Schmeling?

The punch, although it had put Louis off his feet. had not hurt him. Joe was astounded. He was not dazed, not even bleary-eyed. He was up instantly, back at Braddock with a renewed passion tempered with a touch of caution for his continued vulnerability to right hand punches.

"Why didn't you stay down for the nine-count?" Blackburn screamed at Joe in his corner between rounds. "You can't get up so fast that nobody in the place didn't see you was down. And keep on jabbin'. Jab. *Jab!*"

The bell rang for the second round. His confidence bolstered by the first round knockdown, Braddock came out strongly. He threw a flurry of punches. Some landed, some were deflected by Joe's gloves. Braddock continued to press the attack. Louis countered with hard rights. Two punches bounched off Braddock's jaw. He replied with a hard right to Joe's chest . . . grunts and the thud of leather pounding flesh. Louis went after Braddock's head, landed several heavy blows. Pained, Braddock began to strike back wildly. Joe retained his poise. He began to punish the man who held the heavyweight title.

Several still jabs caught Braddock in the third round. One opened a cut over his upper lip. Blood smeared his chin, dripped down on his laboring chest. He appeared near-collapse. His vision seemed to blur beneath the glare of the hot overhead lights, and his body, apparently aching, seemed to summon up resources only the well-trained and brave can muster. Whatever those resources were, whatever inner elixir, they carried the man into the eighth round.

The contest was over. Braddock, an open target for Louis' punishing punches, was functioning purely on courage by the eighth. He pawed the air, trying desperately—by instinct—to reach Louis, and never quite getting there. Instead he moved directly into a right-hand smash to the jaw. The Brown Bomber had put everything into the punch that seemed to split Braddock's face in two. Braddock fell forward, found himself sitting forelornly on the canvas, upper body supported by his right hand. His left arm hung limply, almost as if it were broken or weighed too much to rise up even an inch. Tommy Thomas, the referee, counted him out.

It was not a complicated thing for the 45,000-plus fight fans to understand. And the consequences were equally obvious: Jolting Joe Louis, the Brown Bomber, the black kid from the streets of Chicago and Detroit, was at last heavyweight champion of the world. Still, nothing had really changed significantly . . . either inside the arena or out. On Chicago's South Side, black Americans were charging out of their homes to shout jubilation in the street: *we all knew Joe could do it!* But across the Atlantic was a plague known to the world as Nazism, and although it was a victorious night here in the U.S. for Joe's fans, the victory moved Louis to say, "I don't want nobody to call me champ 'til I beat Schmeling."

2

The long awaited return match with Schmeling, June 22, 1938, if not the highlight of Joe Louis' career, was one of the major high points. Later there would be other dramatic encounters including a heavyweight champion's comeback, an impossibility—so everyone thought—made possible by the omnipotent Brown Bomber and subsequently repeated by Cassius Clay. The news media had their field day at Joe's expense after the first Schmeling fight, some claiming that Louis had lost his "heart" over the knockout by the German and would never again reach that pinnacle of boxing ability achieved before the 1936 defeat. Goebbels and the Nazi propaganda machine, the advent of World War II handwritten on every wall in Western Europe, still made much of the first Schmeling victory. The Nazis mocked the audacity of the black man about to confront Aryan superiority for a second time. It was to be more than a mere prizefight . . . much, much more. Ideologies were about to enter the ring. The Nazis were counting on Schmeling to again prove the theory Hitler was shoving down the Western World's throat, and Franklin D. Roosevelt, spokesman for the American people—particularly black people—was obviously counting on Joe. Never before or since has so much been at stake in the boxing arena.

"Joe, we need muscles like yours to beat Germany," Roosevelt had said. The words whispered themselves in Joe's inner ear as he prepared for the rematch with Schmeling. He and his entourage went to Stevensville, Michigan to rest. In mid-May, the training team was moved to Lafayetteville, New York, where Joe ran a few miles each morning and built up his strength chopping wood. Ready for heavy sparring, the camp returned to Pompton Lakes and the old, familiar training grounds. George Nicholson and Willie Reddish, Joe's major sparring partners, pressed him with hard right-hand punches, the camp determined that the Brown Bomber would not make the same mistake a second time with Schmeling. The weekend sparring sessions attracted as many as five thousand spectators who cluttered the camp with soda pop bottles and bought souvenirs to take home with them. Everyone was watching Joe. Newsmen repeatedly warned him that in Schmeling he would face his most dangerous opponent. "He got to be good," Joe would counter as often as the newsmen voiced their warning. "He knocked me out."

Schmeling was training in the quieter Adirondacks. Max Machon—sharp-nosed, slight of build—was his trainer and confidant. Machon represented the typical

Nazi, an arche-type; he was abrasive, his public comments edged with supremist sarcasm. It was revealed in a German language newspaper that a Nazi uniform hung in Machon's closet in the house where the Schmeling entourage lived. The reporter who made the revelation was Harry Sperber, a refugee from Nazi Germany.

The Nazi propaganda machine continued to crank out trash on both sides of the Atlantic. In Schmeling's camp. Arno Helmer, an official Nazi broadcaster, wired back to Germany that New York's Governor Herbert Lehman was a conspirator in a mass plot to ensure Schmeling's defeat. How this was to be achieved Helmer did not detail. The governor was, after all, a Jew, and everyone laboring under the mental gymnastics of Hitler's philosophy knew about *them*. When Nazi reaction to Helmer's story filtered back to the United States it added fuel to the already raging inferno. There was little love for Schmeling in America. He had taken on the role of villian, and the promoters, particularly Jacobs, were having a field day. Ringside tickets were priced at $40 each. To add even more fuel to the fire, eighteen American citizens were indicted as spies for Nazi Germany. Newspaper headlines across the country carried both stories simultaneously: LOUIS-SCHMELING REMATCH SCHEDULED—NAZI SPIES INDICTED. Still a simple man, Jolting Joe Louis was destined to defend more than the heavyweight crown.

At Pompton Lakes, Louis remained relaxed and concerned only with victory in the ring. Racism, a fact of life every black man confronted daily in America—the Nazis had no market on that scourge—had nothing to do with his personal need to beat Schmeling. Two men were going to fight was all Joe knew. Only one of them would step from the ring as world champion; and, politics and Hitler be damned, Joe was determined to be that man. Both fighters trained to razor-edged perfection. Louis weighed in at 198 3/4, Schmeling at 193.

"There were cops wherever you looked," Joe recalls of the drive to the stadium on the night of the fight. "When we got to the stadium, you could hardly get in. Them bluecoats were everywhere. Going up, we didn't laugh much. Nobody made jokes. It was an important fight."

The fight was indeed more important than a simple man could possibly realize. The crowd, more than 70,000, attested to this. Jacobs, always the promoter and an astute businessman, counted $1,015,012 into his treasury. This was long before contemporary gates that run into the millions. Jacobs had made a fortune through "scalping" ringside seat tickets for as much as $200 each. Even the working press section had provided a source of "black market" revenue for the wily promoter. This section, normally restricted to accredited newsmen, was crowded with Jacobs' *personal* clientele. Some had paid as much as $500 a seat to be close enough to the ring to actually see the tensing muscles and inside blows the sportscasters were to relay over the airways and write about in the morning. More than a prizefight? *Gate* history, as well as poltical history, was being made here.

Louis warmed up in his dressing room. He shadow-boxed himself into a light sweat. When at last he stepped from the dressing room, led by Blackburn and Black and surrounded for protection by a squad of burly policemen, his muscles—the ones FDR had said we Americans needed to beat Germany—glistened beneath the lucky blue and red bathrobe he had worn the first time he fought Schmeling. A roar filled the ballpark when he stepped into the ring. It shook the bleachers. Not since Babe Ruth had driven a homer into the stands during a World Series game years before had such a cacophony of ear-numbing noise been experienced. Fight fans had waited a long time for this night.

Schmeling came draped in an old gray bathrobe. Loud boos gave way to an outburst of cheers. There was a well-established Nazi Bund in the U.S., and there were those who did, in fact, believe the supremist philosophy. Some were present. Even swastickas were seen.

A tentative smile crossed Schmeling's thin lips as he stepped through the ropes. The stadium went suddenly quiet. In the press rows, broadcasters could be heard describing the historical scene. Louis, concentrating on what his handlers were saying, last-minute instructions about that *righthand punch*, began hitting the air with sharp jabs and right crosses, still warming up for the battle that lay only seconds away.

The prefight conference at center ring was brief, Referee Donovan issuing the usual instructions . . . *and no hitting after the bell.* In farmhouses, social and sporting clubs, living rooms and bars across the country, millions inched closer to their radios. In Germany it was 3:00 a.m. Still Arno Helmer's gruff voice was being broadcast over the national network Adolf Hitler's Third Reich maintained.

The bell for the start of round one sounded. A deadly hush fell over the spectator crowd. Those not fortunate enough to have seen Louis in action can never know how it was at the start of one of the Brown Bomber's fights: the shuffling movement—creeping death as he approached his opponent—fists in position, left extended, right hand poised for the kill. You could almost hear the heartbeat of those at ringside as Joe eyed Schmeling, calculating. The German backed cautiously away. Louis pushed two jabs into the man's face, stalking. Schmeling took several quick steps backward and Louis moved in.

The German caught Joe with a punch to the head. Instead of hurting Louis, it was like a sudden release. The blow landed by Schmeling seemed to dissipate the tension, leaving Joe to unwind into the superbly trained fighting machine honed at Pompton Lakes. He landed several left hooks and a smashing righthand to Schmeling's jaw. The crowd came out of its seats. The German was hurt . . . my God, how many seconds had passed?

Schmeling retreated to the ropes, right arm hooked over the top strand. He rested his chin on his forearm, trying desperately to shake off the blows. He was three-quarters exposed. Louis hit him with both gloves giving hard, telling rights, lefthand flurries. Far out into the ballpark, the sound went berserk. Referee Donovan stepped between the two, started the count. To onlookers, it seemed that Schmeling was already out on his feet.

Staggering, obviously groggy, the German somehow managed to move toward center ring. The noise of the crowd shook the stadium in one long piercing scream. Louis was on Schmeling again, first with a left, and then a mind-boggling right to the jaw. This time, dazed and pained, a caricature of the man who had faced Louis in the first fight, the German went down. He took a three count, came up. But Louis was still there, waiting, nostrils flaring. His face was a mask of grim determination. Both gloves pounded Schmeling's head. Again the German went down, this time slowly, softly. Knees bent as if his 193 pounds were too much to bear. His gloves touched the canvas lightly.

A towel—once the recognized sign of surrender in

boxing but no longer valid in New York State—was flung into the ring by Machon. The referee, still counting over the fallen German, kicked the soggy thing backward. It hit the ropes and hung as forelornly as Schmeling had done seconds earlier, this time over the middle strand. Donovan counted to five. Then, apparently realizing that the German was finished, stopped the fight. It had lasted two minutes and four seconds—a first round knockout by the audacious black man who dared confront Aryan superiority a second time.

Louis, usually so passive of expression, so noncommittal, allowed himself the pleasure of a smile as he returned to his corner. Fans and the Louis entourage leaped into the ring screaming congratulations. Everyone wanted to be close to the powerful champion, to share in the victory.

Joe sat on his stool, the sweat of combat making his brown body glisten beneath the hot overhead lights. He watched as Schmeling, still dazed, came across the ring to drape one arm over the black champion's enormous shoulder and grin crookedly. There was no doubt now, none whatsoever.

In Nazi Germany, Helmer's description of the end of the fight was never heard. Somebody, it seemed, immediately as Schmeling went down for the first time, had pulled the master switch that controlled the Third Reich's radio network.

Much, much more than a mere prizefight had been fought in the stadium this night!

Later, in his dressing room, Louis was surrounded by newsmen asking their pointed questions. Some wanted him to comment on the racial and political ramifications of the bout. Others wanted to know if he hated Schmeling, either for knocking him out in the first fight—

that controversial blow after the bell—or for being a Nazi. The championship was secure. The rest still to be pending thousands of miles away.

"I opened him up with left jabs," Joe said.

That was all. Joe Louis refused to claim that he had singlehandedly disproved Hitler's theory of a master race. He remained a simple man, a black prizefighter. But now, HEAVYWEIGHT CHAMPION OF THE WORLD flashed on both sides of the Atlantic. Many people came to his dressing room that night. One was Frank Murphy, governor of Joe's home state of Michigan.

"Michigan is proud of you," Murphy said in an emotion packed tone of voice.

It was true. Lots of people all over the world were proud of the Brown Bomber that night.

"Thanks," was all Joe had to say in reply.

Afterward, following the shower that wiped the sweat of battle from his body, Joe returned to Harlem. He rode in a limousine through the streets filled with his shouting fans. The celebration was nationwide, but crested in New York's Harlem where Schmeling was an ugly symbol who had been crushed by a black man. Joe Louis felt only the victory won with his hands. Others around him felt more . . . much, much more.

Marva was waiting for him at a friend's apartment on Saint Nicholas Avenue. There would be no bad dreams this night, no nightmares of Nazi fists pummelting Joe's face. She had won $15 on the bout, betting her man would knock Schmeling out in four rounds. It was a good feeling. The hard training was over and done for a while, victory complete. But then, Joe had always been her special black champion.

Next day, Joe went to Mike Jacobs' office to talk to

the promoter and reporters. Mike told him that his share of the purse was $349,228. Joe was, of course, pleased . . . a simple man with all that money! Most of all he was pleased that he had wiped out the memory of that first fight with Schmeling. The championship was authentic now, no one could claim otherwise. Jolting Joe Louis, the black kid from the streets of Detroit and Chicago, was unrefutably *the champ*. He was making more money than he had ever dreamed of. The future looked bright for a 23-year-old black dude who had never done much in the way of education but sure as hell had fought his way up the ladder to boxing stardom. What lay ahead could now only be better than what had gone down before.

Joe sat passively in Mike's office barely thinking about what Roosevelt had said to him at the White House: "We need muscles like yours to beat Germany, Joe."

Joe's battle was not with the Nazis, no way. His battle had to do with being a black champion in a world that took advantage of black men of good will.

Munroe Barrow, Joe Louis' father with three of his eight children. When Joe was two his father was committed to an Alabama state hospial for the emotionally disturbed.

3

Like so many other black men who had and would later achieve fame in the ring, Joe Louis had humble beginnings. Born May 13, 1914 in Cusseta, Alabama, Joe was the seventh child of the Barrow family. He weighed almost eleven pounds at birth—a strapping baby. Joe came from a long line of "big" people, mostly blacks, some white mixed in, and a few powerful Indians. It made for healthy stock in the lad destined to become heavyweight champion of the world.

Number thirteen—Joe's birthday—is traditionally an unlucky number. "But old people always say there's something lucky about the number seven," Joe claims.

Indeed, the seventh child born to Munrow Barrow and Lily Reese Barrow was the only one in the family to achieve the heights of acclaim that characterized Joe's boxing career. No one would have guessed what the boy's destiny was from the place where he romped as a youngster. There was nothing "lucky" about being born in Cusseta. It was a red clay place. Sometimes, as a boy with impressionable eyes, Joe thought the whole world was made up of the red stuff. The red hills of Cusseta ran into the mountains, and the mountains ran twelve miles into Lafayette, Alabama. A red clay road ran off another road called "Cusseta," and Cusseta led off toward the Buckalew Mountain section. Not much of a place for a champion to be nourished. Not even a proper living room, nine people, seven of them kids, living wherever they could all over the house. It was difficult for Joe, for anyone, to see beyond the cotton balls and those hard red hills.

Like most of the area's residents, especially the black folks, the Barrows were hard-working farmers. It was difficult, and sometimes near impossible, to till the red clay soil of Cusseta. Yet, not only did the Barrows till the soil, they grew the cotton, picked it, baled it up, and sold it. With the exception of his teacher and the area doctor, everyone Joe knew as a boy was a poor dirt farmer. Even the minister donned bib overalls and farmer's garb six days a week, and on Sunday at the Mt. Sinai Baptist Church three miles from the Barrow home, gave a homespun farmer's sermon.

"I didn't figure on anything except I'd be a farmer, a husband, a father, and that's about it," Joe admitted in his autobiography: *Joe Louis: My Life,* published by Harcourt Brace Jovanovich, Inc. in 1978.

It was a hard life for Joe as a youngster. The years of strain and constant work had put Munrow Barrow in the epileptic ward of Searcy Hospital for the Negro Insane at Mt. Vernon, Alabama, when Joe was barely two years old. That, in itself, was no disgrace: many hard-working black men had literally worked themselves into a stupor or death in the South, and Munrow was a *good* man. Joe remembers his momma saying that their daddy had rented the 120-acre farm thinking he could thereby provide an adequate living for his growing family, and he had failed—the snapping point! He had left the farm to be run by Joe's great-uncle, Peter Sheley. Still, Munrow escaped from the hospital from time to time to visit with his family until he was caught, and Joe recalls one such escape, a visit that lasted more than two years.

When, at last, Munrow finally stopped escaping from the hospital, someone told Mrs. Barrow that her husband was dead. She believed it. He was dead to her and the children in any case. There were nine hungry mouths to feed—another daughter had come along after Joe—and hard times, harder than most folks can imagine, on a poor red clay farm in Cusseta. Neighbors tried as best they could to help. Many sent Joe on simple errands so he could earn pennies and sometimes as much as a nickle which he gave eagerly to "momma."

"God, I loved that woman," Joe recalls. "Her face was honey-brown, sweet and pleasant. Don't get me wrong though. Momma could mix it up some, too. She could be tough. You stepped out of line with her and she'd put your head between her knees and whup you with a strap. One thing, though, nobody around could say the Barrow children were wild or bad or didn't have any manners."

Somehow Momma Lily Barrow managed to meet up with a man named Patrick Brooks after word circulated that Munrow was dead. Pat was a sharecropper, a widower, with eight children of his own. There was Momma Barrow with her eight kids—baby-sister

Vunice born shortly after Joe—and Pat Brooks with his clan. They decided to get married.

Sixteen children living in the same house. It was hectic, the way Joe remembers it: a cliche, but never a dull moment. Pat was, however, the only father Joe ever really knew, and he was a good, God-fearing, hardworking man—an excellent influence. Both the Barrow house and Pat's home were a mite small for sixteen kids, so the combined families moved into a bigger place at Camp Hill, deeper into the Buckalew Mountains.

A sort of rivalry developed between Joe and Pat Brooks, Jr., a stepbrother the same age as Joe. One day, Joe recalls, Pat picked up a brick and hit him in the head. He still carries the scar. Joe was barely eight years old, but already he seemed to have developed a knack for *getting into tussles* with Pat and other boys from the area. He would fight when he played marbles, but only if they "bothered him." And if any of the boys bothered one of his sisters, well . . . ! There was a fighting game they played called "knocking" where Joe would put a chip of wood on his shoulder and dare the older boys to knock it off. If anyone dared, there was a fight. "But most times it was more noise and running and throwing stones than anything else," Joe recalls in retrospect. Boys will be boys, and future prizefight champions are perhaps even more so.

Throughout his career, people have persisted in asking Joe about those early days in Alabama. The South, notorious for its racist philosophies and anti-black practices, must have had some effect on the young Louis, most fans reason aloud. Some have wondered if the *crackers* gave Joe a hard time while he was coming up in Cusseta. "Did the Ku Klux Klan ever bother you or your family?" one such curious fan once put to Joe at an inverview.

"To tell the honest, absolute truth, there didn't seem to be anything bad between blacks and whites in Alabama," Joe replied. "But you have to remember I was a little boy. There were other things that I did not take a hold to. I remember black people getting together and talking about how much white blood they had, how much Indian blood they had, but hardly heard anyone would talk about how much black blood they had. I didn't know too much, but I could easily see that all these white-blooded, Indian-blooded black people lived a damn sight worse than some of the poorest white people I saw. I knew there was a difference, but it made no difference to me."

As Joe remembers, he and his family, including the Brooks family, got along well with the white people in Alabama. In retrospect, it was sort of a "black folks had their place, white folks had theirs" system of getting along.

"Probably we never crossed the line to cause the angers and hurts and lynchings that took place all over the South," Joe reflects. "One thing . . . nobody white ever called me a 'nigger' until I got to Detroit."

Detroit! The first time Joe ever heard of the place was when some of Pat Brooks' relatives came down to the Buckalew Mountains for a visit. It sounded to Joe, and to Pat and Momma and the rest of the family, like another world altogether, everyone talking about cars, jobs in factories, and money. Mostly money. Steady pay. The jobs in Detroit did not depend on rainfall or the habits of the boll weevil. Folks got their pay every week—even black folks—and for the first time in his young life Joe heard about stone sidewalks, movies and indoor electricity. Of course, he and the other children had known about the invention of electricity, and had even seen it work, but they had never seen it inside their own home and the thought was exciting. Their light came from kerosene lamps that smelled and filled the house with thick black smoke. Besides, what did poor sharecroppers need with electricity when just about everyone was in bed by sundown, up at dawn, and too damned tired to do much more than sleep through the darkness between.

The decision was made. The combined Brooks/Barrow families could not do any worse by relocating, and just might do better. The visiting relatives had said that the Ford factory in Detroit didn't mind hiring Negroes, and the promise of a weekly paycheck was almost too good to be true. Pat Brooks, Joe's Momma and the other boys from both families packed and trekked off to Detroit to have a good look around for themselves before uprooting the entire household. It was to be the turning point in the young Brown Bomber's life.

From the red clay of Cusseta and the Buckalew Mountain region to Detroit was a long train ride. It had taken a year for Patrick Brooks and Momma Barrow to save enough money to get the rest of the family up North. Down home everyone said, "Negroes up North are smart," Joe remembers. Now he watched out the train window as the cities got bigger, the houses taller. He watched the chain gang workers along the grading, noted the striped uniforms they wore—just like in the movies. He remembered what his momma had told him about being good and about what could happen if he were bad. No sir, not for him. He would never be chained like those black men along the side of the tracks. Somewhere, perhaps in Detroit, there had to be something better for him. One thing certain, he wouldn't be seeing any more red clay hills and cotton fields.

Detroit was a wonder for a twelve-year-old country

boy seeing it for the first time. There had never been so many people in one place, so many cars. There were no trolley cars in Cusseta—another marvel—and here there were parks, brick schoolhouses, movie theaters and libraries. People dressed differently too: city dress. In his new overalls and country shoes, Joe felt awkward. Still, Detroit looked awfully good to him.

There were too many new things to count. There was the house on Madison Avenue equipped with electric lights to pull on and off at whim, and an indoor toilet that flushed when you pulled the chain. There were so many good things. Some bad things, too.

Joe had never heard of "gangs" before. Not gangs as we know them today . . . the Chicanos against the blacks, the blacks against whitey, etc. These exist in most big cities. But back in Detroit when Joe was twelve, the *gangs* were the beginnings of what has since come to be known as The Syndicate or The Organization. There was the infamous Purple Gang near where Joe and his family lived, a tough bunch comprised of mostly Jewish boys. The connections stretched to Louisiana and out to Chicago where Al Capone reigned as chieftain. They operated from the Detroit River, and sometimes Joe could see the police trucks confiscating bootleg liquor and stolen goods. Occasionally, Joe and his family watched the police cart away the remains of a murder victim—what would later come to be known as "a hit." Detroit was full of new things, some more than enough to make a twelve-year-old's head spin.

The depression came along just when things were beginning to look grand. If there is an economic indicator for hard times, it has to be black folks losing their jobs—the first to go! One by one, Joe's brothers and stepfather lost theirs, and for the first time in his life, the young future champion went hungry. Things got so bad for a time that Joe did not have shoes to wear to school, and several concerned teachers donated clothes for the family. Worse, Joe could not keep up with his classmates. He was bigger than anybody but just couldn't seem to get past the sixth grade. Even Vunice, his younger sister, caught up to and passed him by. One thing was dramatically clear. If fortune and fame was to befall Joe Louis, it would have nothing to do with reading, writing and 'rithmatic.

One of the more observant teachers at Duffield School came to the obvious conclusion that Joe had better educate his hands instead of his head, and he was transferred to Bronson, an all-boys vocational school. He began to do woodwork. He liked the change, and it was a way to furnish the house during hard times, bringing home the tables and cabinets and shelves he made for the family's approval. Still, times were tough. Eventually the family had to go on the Depression "soup line."

Joe remembers his momma having to go down to the local relief office once a week and wait in line to get the family some money. There was never much during those days . . . *talkin' 'bout hard times,* a la Ray Charles. But Joe is proud to say today that after he fought Charley Massera in 1934, he paid back every penny of the $400-odd his family received from the relief office during that bleak period.

Joe had made a friend in Freddie Guinyard, a skinny little guy who worked the Eastern Vegetable and Produce Market, taking odd jobs, moving vegetables about—just about anything to make money. What Joe remembers most about Freddie is the day he was sent home from school because a teacher had said—only to the colored kids—that anyone who made good grades would be rewarded by getting a chance to shine shoes at

Hudson's Department Store on weekends, and Freddie had jumped right up, and asked, "Why would you need to have good grades to shine shoes?" The teacher's answer was to dismiss Freddie from class. It was the first time Joe began to think about racial matters.

Everything seems to cost an enormous amount of money when you are broke, and everyone in the Brooks/Barrow clan was trying as best they could to put food in the family stomach. Some had married off, and would help, like sister Emmarell, by giving Joe odd jobs to do to supplement. Freddie and Joe went into business of sorts—a job on an ice wagon, delivering blocks of ice in the days before poor folks could afford refrigerators or freezers. They trucked around Detroit in a horse-drawn wagon, burlap over the ice to keep it from melting.

"But it wasn't all hard times and scraping to get by," Joe recalls. "I had some good times, too."

On Saturdays, they used to go to the Catherine Theater, Joe remembers. He loved movies, still does, particularly the cowboy movies staring Buck Jones, Ken Maynard, Tom Mix and the other all-time greats. Detroit still held many wonders for Joe, many adventures that had a way of making the bad times not so bad. He was older now, seventeen. And there were girls: he had always loved beautiful girls. He had him one, too. The family would have frowned upon the relationship had they known, because Bennie Franklin, the girl, was one of Joe's older sister's stepdaughters. Still the relationship lasted from the time Joe was 14 until he was almost married. The way he broke up with Bennie—a call from New Jersey the day before the Max Baer fight to tell her he was getting married—is one of Joe's few romantic regrets, but a sweetness he still savors amid the memories of the Depression.

Momma, too, had decided that Joe needed something for a future. Somewhere, somehow, she had heard about a music teacher in the area, and thought that might be for Joe. She sent him to take violin lessons at fifty cents a class—a lot of money in those days—plus the rental fee for the violin. There he was—six feet tall, big as a light heavyweight—carrying his violin, until some guy at the Bronson School called him a sissy and he smashed the silly little violin over the boy's head.

Thus ended the violin period. There was a guy at school named Thurston McKinney who had just won the 1932 Golden Gloves in Detroit for the 147-pound division, and he and Joe became friends. Momma still insisted that Joe practice violin, although his heart had gone out of it long before the head-smashing episode. One day Thurston talked Joe into accompanying him to Brewster's East Side Gymnasium instead of attending the scheduled violin lesson class. It was the beginning of great things to come. Like looking into a crystal ball, that first impulsive visit to a professional gym—the violin secreted in a locker paid for with his music lesson money—showed young Louis the way to obtaining his future.

With its exercise apparatus, the ring, speed and punching bag, mats and pulleys, the gym was as much a wonder to Joe as his first exposure to Detroit. He worked out in borrowed trunks and an old pair of tennis shoes. Soon he became a regular at Brewster's East Side Gymnasium, and Atler Ellis, the man who ran the place, offered to show Joe how to box. It was not long after that Thurston McKenney asked the young Bomber to be his sparring partner.

"He beat me all over the ring," Joe admits. "He hit me with a right to the jaw that almost dropped me. I got mad. I let go my right. It caught him on the chin. His eyes got glassy and his knees buckled, and if I hadn't moved fast to hold him up, I would have knocked him out . . . and he was the Golden Glove Lightweight Champion of Detroit."

Thurston merely shook his head. Then he grinned, and said, "Man, throw that violin away."

According to Joe, there is no expressing how he felt at that fateful moment, no way to adequately describe it. He felt a new power surging through his arms and fists. It was like "sudden religion," seeing the light. Sure, there had been street fights in his life, but this was not fighting because he was angry with someone or protecting his sisters. This was *professional*.

There was scheming to be done. At last, Joe knew what he wanted to do with his life, but there was "momma" and the fifty cents given to him for the violin lessons that was being spent on locker rental. There was more money needed. Trunks and equipment that fit properly had not been used. He went to Emmarell, his sister. She donated what she could and promised not to tell momma until he worked something out with this new prizefighting adventure. That too was solved for him when he arrived home from the gym one Saturday and found the violin teacher there talking to Momma. There was no getting around it. Joe did not want to continue the violin lessons, the teacher admitted that he had no talent, and Momma swallowed hard at the admission that her baby boy wanted to make his way in the world through punching people's lights out in the ring.

"No matter what you do," Momma told him after the violin teacher had left, "remember you're from a Christian family, and always act that way."

That was that! Although unhappy about the decision,

both Momma and Patrick had agreed that if any of their children wanted something badly enough, they'd see to it that they were granted at least a chance. The violin lessons had ended on the day Joe smashed the instrument over the loud-mouth's head, but now it was official . . . sanctioned by Momma.

Talk of big money generated conversations between Joe and Thurston. The latter began to show Joe pictures of Jack Dempsey, Jack Johnson and Kid Chocolate in the fight magazines. These fighters were making it *big*, more money than Joe had ever dreamed of. The thought of some of that money made Joe's head spin.

Now, when Joe was not working or in school, he could be found at the gym. He trained religiously. The sudden career aspiration had gained him the respect of friends and neighbors. Everyone already knew he could fight because Pat, his stepbrother, often called Joe to handle a bully for him. Joe always won. It got to the point where Pat's enemies often declined at the mere sight of the burly young Bomber. There was that and the Catherine Street Gang, fifty tough guys. Although neither Joe nor his brothers were members, they often fought when the gang was protecting the neighborhood against intruders. They fought with their fists, no weapons. Joe had already established a reputation as a good, hard puncher, and now the steady workouts at the gym enhanced that reputation even more.

Most of the Catherine Street Gang eventually ended in jail. Fortunately for Joe, he and his brothers went a different way. The young Bomber was too busy with fighting in the ring to worry about street gangs. Plus there was Benny Mitchell with whom to wile away his hours outside the gym.

Alter Ellis watched and became interested in Joe. He recruited Holman Williams, a black middleweight, to help train the ambitious lad. Holman was not much older than Joe, but he was already an amateur fighter who would later turn pro.

Ironically, Joe's stepfather could see no future for the boy as a prizefigher and constantly tried talking to his stepson about a steady job. Momma, on the other hand, said, "If you want to be a fighter, be one." It was a tug-o'-war until Joe brought Thurston home to talk to the folks about the merchandise checks an amateur boxer received. With Pat Brooks out of work and hard times still upon the combined family, the idea of those checks made boxing much more appealing.

Soon, everyone knew that Joe could punch your lights out . . . if he could catch you. There was much to learn. Joe had found that there was no such thing as a "natural" in the ring. It was a science, lots of hard work and sweat. "A natural dancer has to practice hard," Joe once said. "A natural painter has to paint all the time. Even a natural fool has to work at it."

Young Joe Louis had the God-given talent to be a professional prizefighter. But it had to be honed, sharpened up. Only a natural fool would have thought otherwise.

Joe Louis was already immensely popular when he married Marva Trotter a few minutes before he knocked out Max Baer on September 24, 1935 before 90,000 fans at Yankee Stadium.

4

Joe felt he was ready. Against the advice of Holman Williams, a fighter who encouraged Joe and was his friend, the Bomber talked Alter Ellis into setting up a match with Johnny Miler, a white boy who had been on the Olympic boxing team in Los Angeles in 1932. Miler was experienced and tough, perhaps the best the light heavyweight amateur division had to offer. Williams, who had fought several bouts with Miler, insisted that Joe was going in over his head. But Joe had seen a photograph of Miler and there was something about the way the man posed that had convinced the Brown Bomber that the white boy could be beaten. Joe was certain. He knew he could do it. It was going to be the start of his chosen career.

Still, Joe did not want his family to know that he was finally entering the ring. He dropped the name "Barrow." It the fight were publicized, if it got into the local papers, Momma and the family would read about Joe Louis fighting Miler and never be the wiser.

Feeling good, feeling fine, certain of victory, Joe entered the ring at the Naval Armory in Detroit. It was going to be his big day. He even had his own cheering section—Thurston, Holman, Atler Ellis, and his friend Freddie Guinyard. The bout was scheduled for three rounds. Miler knocked him down several times in two. Miler won. Joe lost. Holman Williams had been right. Miler was too far ahead of Joe in everything.

"Next time, jab with your left before shooting the right," both Holman and Atler advised. Then, reassuring the crestfallen Bomber, "Anybody who can get up seven times got to have something going for them."

Indeed, the young and determined Joe Louis had something. Part of it was the deadly right punch that put opponent after opponent on the canvas during sparring sessions. The biggest problem, it seemed, was lack of ring experience. That and over-eagerness had caused him to step back and drop his guard once the right punch landed, leaving Miler enraged and coming at him with both gloves flying. Joe went home that night with a badly wounded ego. His momma cried when she saw the effects of the beating.

Unsure of himself after the Miler fight, his pride wounded by seven knockdowns, Joe allowed Poppa Brooks to talk him into a "steady job." Poppa Brooks was getting to be an old man, he told the young, would-be prizefighter, and aside from marrying Joe's momma and getting out of Alabama, he hadn't accomplished very much in his life. Perhaps Joe should settle down, take that steady job at the Ford plant and find a nice girl to marry. It would be better than coming home looking like something a ragged cat might drag in.

"The way I ached and the way my feelings hurt, Poppa's advice sounded good," Joe later claimed. He did, in fact, take the job at the Ford facotry at River Rouge for $25 a week. He stayed away from the gym for a full two months.

It was Joe's first real job, the first time in his life he had to devote a certain number of hours for a certain amount of pay. He got what he considered the hardest job the factory had to offer . . . *pushing* truck bodies to a conveyor belt. It was no fun. Sometimes after work Joe's back hurt so badly that he simply could not straighten up.

The new job didn't last very long. Joe began to figure that if he was going to hurt that much for $25 a week, he could do just as well through trying the ring again. His wounded pride had begun to heal itself, and the old eagerness, the itch that had put him against Johnny Miler ahead of his time, was gnawing again. He left the Ford factory in January, 1933, and never returned.

When Joe stepped into Brewster's East Side Gymnasium for the first time in two months, paused to watch the boys working the speed and punching bags, got the scent in his nostrils—a combination of sweat, the leather of gloves and canvas—he wondered why he had ever allowed Poppa Brooks to persuade him to stop. Boxing was in his blood. He felt at home here, the grunts and the thuds of gloves pounding flesh had somehow become an integral part of his makeup. He knew, too, that he wanted big money. That, to Joe, the simple farm boy, meant $60 to $70 a week. He had his fill of what most folks called a "regular" job. There was no way he could make his big money in that. Here in the gym, in the ring, there was at least a chance to do better.

Holman Williams became Joe's trainer. He worked hard with Joe because, as he and Ellis had said, the young Louis "had to have something to get up seven times." This time Joe trained more seriously. He stayed away from friends and running around. He ate as well as he could, slept soundly. He was learning fast, faster than most, but not quite fast enough for Joe.

Ellis watched as Williams trained. he could see the potential power in Joe's right hand—the killer punch. He also saw that Joe was not using his left to full capacity, which was the flaw in Joe Louis' early career. One day Ellis said he wanted to try something and got Joe to go along. He tied the younger Bomber's right to the corner of the ring, put Thurston McKinney in with him. The bell sounded. Thurston proceeded to lay into Joe.

"Tie me loose," Joe shouted in frustration as Thurston beat the hell out of him.

Ellis merely laughed. It was a forced practice maneuver. It made Joe use his left hand to ward off Thurston, and supposedly taught him the importance of the weapon he had somehow neglected to train up to par.

Soon after his return to the gym Holman arranged a three-round amateur bout between Joe and Otis Thomas at the Forest Athletic Club in Detroit. Joe was less spunky this time. He climbed into the ring remembering Miler. Would this fighter knock him all over the place, too? He wondered. Use him? Send him home with a shattered pride a second time?

Not this time, Joe promised himself as the bell sounded for the first round. He tucked in his chin, shuffled forward . . . the beginnings of the classic Joe Louis style. It ended in round one: a left hook and a right to the jaw, and Thomas was out. Joe was on top of the world again. He had scored the first official knockout of his career.

After the Thomas bout, there were thirteen straight knockouts in Joe's career. He was learning fast and getting good. Fight promoters around the amateur circles were beginning to give him a second look, and asking for him as an opponent more and more. The merchandise checks kept rolling in, $25 a bout. At home, Momma and Poppa were beginning to look at the fight game with a different eye.

The next big step was Golden Gloves. There would be no more merchandising checks, only medals and trophies, but it was the last phase of training before going professional. Joe's world was getting bigger, his prospects more lucrative. The Detroit Free Press sent him to Chicago to fight Clinton Bridges, a Golden Glove heavyweight. Bridges beat him on points—a minor irritation and momentary setback. Then Boston where he was outpointed again, this time by Max Marek in the National Amateur Championship. Marek, star of the Notre Dame football team, hadn't knocked him out: an encouraging factor, outpointed or not. It spurred Joe on to six victories in a row in the National Amateur Championship Tournament. True, he had lost a few, but he was winning more than he was losing and over some really tough opponents. It was a new and exciting life. He was away from home and family for the first time, getting to know the guys around the amateur circle, and enjoying himself while laying the groundwork for his career.

Holman backed out of the training schedule. A fighter himself, his own career to consider, he could not keep up with Joe. He recommended a new trainer, George Slayton, who ran the Detroit Athletic Club.

Joe was moving fast all right, but not fast enough for his ambitions. It was December, 1933, he was nineteen years old, and there was another black heavyweight who was becoming popular in and around Detroit. Stanley Evans was his name. He was strong in the ring, but Slayton thought Joe was ready, and Joe did too. The fight was booked. As it turned out, Joe was *not* ready. Evans outpointed him. Another defeat, another lesson learned about patience and the science of boxing.

Slayton's faith in Joe's ability was not diminished by the loss. He introduced the young fighter to Mr. Roxborough, a tall, light-skinned black man who dressed well, spoke softly, and exuded class. Roxborough was interested in Joe. So much so that he asked Joe to come around to his real estate office for a talk. Roxborough had a reputation for helping people, going as far as sending some to college. The real estate office was, of course, a front, Roxborough being one of the biggest numbers men in Detroit. It was days of hard living for black folks in the Depression. Anyone smart enough to own his own numbers operation was smart enough to be kind and giving in the black neighborhood. Roxborough got as much respect as a doctor or lawyer, and it was kind of a blast for Joe to know that a man so important was interested in him. Roxborough's brother Charlie was a lawyer, politician, and a big wheel in the Urban League and the Young Negro Progressive Association. Mr. Roxborough was surrounded by dignity and legitimacy.

Roxborough knew that Joe was hurting financially, needed things. Without batting an eye, Joe recalls, the big time numbers man took the young prizefighter to Long's Drugstore and told the owner to charge to *his* account anything Joe needed. Not much—clean bandages, rubbing alcohol and such, but impressive. Plus there were meals at the Roxborough home. Mrs. Roxborough, good-looking and gracious, smiled as she served him. Joe had never before seen black folks living so well. He was envious.

Roxborough's gift of a new pair of boxing gloves left Joe speechless. It was the *coup de grace* to the hand-me-down clothes and pocket money the generous backer had already given. It made Joe work even harder, train more doggedly. His reputation was growing, and there was an important match, a Golden Gloves light heavyweight bout, coming up in Chicago. It was good to have a backer. Joe was feeling good, feeling fine.

On the night of the big fight, Joe sat in his dressing room with his new professional gloves, ready to take on the world if he had to, a commotion started outside the door. Suddenly a group of detectives barged in. "You're under arrest," they told him. "We're taking you to the Eleventh Street Police Station."

Scared, more frightened than he had ever been in his life, Joe went along and tried desperately to think of what he had done to be arrested for. The charges were read to him at the station house. He wanted to laugh but was still scared. He was being held on the charge of murdering *his wife* in Gary, Indiana, in 1929. Joe kept trying to tell them that he was only fifteen at the time and never married. . . a mistake? The investigation went forward. . . legitimate error? Finally, amid grunts of apology, he was released, but too late for the scheduled fight. Later, Mr. Roxborough learned that some Chicago "fight fans" had been watching Joe train and probably thought he could beat his opponent. They had the whole thing *arranged* so that their man would not suffer a defeat.

The incident gave Joe a greater sense of his own importance. He was now a threat to other boxers, a menacing entity lurking in the background. He became more determined and trained hard for his rematch with Evans. There was a sweet life somewhere ahead on the boxing horizon. He meant to get there however long it took. He fought Evans again in 1934, and this time he beat him to win the light heavyweight crown for the Detroit Golden Gloves.

Joe's last amateur fight was in Ford Field, Detroit. It was an inter-city light heavyweight competition that was over in two minutes. The opponent's name was Joe Bauer. Joe knocked him out on June 12, 1934 . . . a red-letter day in the Brown Bomber's career. After the fight, Mr. Roxborough said, "I think you're ready, Joe. Time to turn professional."

Joe was excited and nervous. It was time! Roxborough said he had great faith in Joe, and that he would do far better careerwise in Chicago with Julian Black as his manager. Joe had come to depend on Roxborough, not only for the money and clothes and essentials that were always there since he'd met the man, but for friendship, too. Roxborough assured Joe that he would always be around, could be contacted at any time. Then he told Joe some interesting facts about Julian Black.

At one time, Mr. Roxborough himself had been in financial trouble with his numbers business. Julian Black had bailed him out of a tight situation with a lot of front money. Now that Roxborough was doing well again, he wanted to return the favor. That was one reason for the merger. Another reason, an even more important one, was that Julian Black had a stable of black fighters in Chicago, and plenty of money because he was a high-rolling numbers operator also. "You can't ever really be a big success without having money," Mr. Roxborough advised. "Or at least having someone to give it to you."

Joe was a bit nervous about leaving home and friends, young and hardheaded, too. Mr. Roxborough was patient. A few days after the Bauer fight he told Joe about the fate of most black fighters, those with white men for managers, how they ended burned out and broken before they reached their prime because the white managers were not interested in the men, only in the money that could be made from them. They—the white managers—according to Roxborough, did not take time to see that their black fighters were trained properly before entering the ring. They were not concerned that the black fighters ate properly, lived comfortably, and had pocket change. White and black did not seem to mix in the fight game . . . black men were merely used to line the white managers' pockets with purse money. Mr. Roxborough was talking about Black Power before it became a popular topic of black conversation.

"Okay, I'm ready," Joe finally agreed. "But you have to come by an' tell my momma."

Roxborough laughed. Next day he was there at the Brooks/Barrow home to talk to Momma Barrow and Poppa Brooks about Joe's career. He told them the things he had told Joe, about black prizefighters being used by white men, burning out and such. Momma, always concerned about her "baby" boy's lifestyle, agreed to let Roxborough send him off to Chicago. "If you make sure he lives well," she amended. "If you make sure he leads a decent Christian life."

Roxborough agreed. Poppa Brooks added, "Fighting was all right when Joe used to get those merchandise checks regular. But who can eat all those trophies he's bringing home now? Might as well try to make some money."

Roxborough assured them there was money to be made, more than even Joe dreamed of. The fight game was more than bloody noses and swollen features, gruelling schedules and hard training. There was a world of luxury and wealth waiting for the man who could punch his way to the heavyweight championship of the world, and Roxborough was convinced that Joe at least had a chance at it. He, Roxborough, had the charm and intelligence needed to convince Momma and Poppa. Joe could go now with their blessing. He would have gone anyway, but now he could do it with an easy conscience.

It was hardest on Bennie. Six years is a long time to be in love and keep it a secret. Joe told her it was going to be great; he was going to make lots of money, then they'd tell the world and nobody, but *nobody*, could do anything about it.

Like leaving Alabama way back when, the young Louis felt scared and happy at the same time. "Chicago look out," was Joe's thought upon leaving Detroit. He was a *comer* and knew it.

5

An agreement was reached immediately when Joe arrived in Chicago: Louis would turn professional under the guidance of two men. Jack Blackburn was hired as Joe's trainer. Julian Black was the second man in the agreement.

Louis soon learned to respect Blackburn. "He called me 'Chappie,' and I called him Chappie," Joe would later say. "Whatever he told me to do in the ring, I did. I used to be clumsy-footed when I was a kid in Alabama. When I began with Blackburn, he saw things I didn't know about myself. He saw I couldn't follow a left hook with a right without picking up one foot. He said it was no good, that a fighter had to keep both feet planted on the canvas to get power, or to take a punch.

He soon had me throwing a series of punches. He was the best teacher anybody ever had.''

Louis no longer ate hot dogs. He lived in the apartment of Bill Bottoms, a chef who cooked for Joe. Later, Bottoms would become the cook in the Louis training camp. Blackburn, a stern trainer with lots of experience, looked the part. He had a bony face, marked by a scar on the left cheek and set off by beady eyes that stared out at you through slits. He appeared to be a disciplinarian, and was. Usually taciturn, he was informative and kind where Joe was concerned. He saw boxing as a serious business that demanded a man's undivided attention. If Joe Louis was going to be good, a contender, that philosophy had to sink in. It was a jealous profession. When a fighter broke training, made the profession secondary, it was more deadly than a woman scorned. Louis' career as a professional fighter was about to begin, and he could not have been in more competent hands. Joe was pleased, and mostly happy. Yet at the back of his mind smoldered the influences that would lead, years later, to darkest despair.

But now was *now*, and there was no inkling of the mental stress that lay ahead. Joe had been to Chicago before and knew what to expect from the city. Roxborough and Black had helped him settle in with Bottoms, and for the first time in Joe's life he was to have a room to himself. There were many firsts happening to him since he'd met Roxborough. He would learn the meaning of privacy, learn to love it and sometimes hate it. Roxborough and Black talked business constantly, most of which Joe didn't understand. Joe looked out the apartment window and saw Washington Park. It was where he would do his roadwork for the next year.

Suddenly the conversation between Roxborough and Black ended. Black looked hard at Joe. ''Your first professional fight will be in little over a month," he informed Joe.

There was lots of money being invested in Joe, and Black told him that they expected him to make a big investment in himself. It was going to be a gruelling pace: training would be hard and long so that he would be ready. Black was going to drop most of his other fighters and concentrate almost exclusively on Joe. Blackburn was going to be there at all times to make sure Joe adhered to the rigid schedule.

Blackburn! Joe remembers him as the man whose superior knowledge of boxing and God-given talent made him, Louis, the first black man to become heavyweight champion of the world since Jack Johnson in 1915.

Blackburn had been born in Kentucky in 1893. He was something of a fighter himself in his own day: over 100 bouts in a twenty-year career. He had won most of them. He was a lightweight in poundage, but a heavy in character and style. He had served five years in prison on a murder charge, and he was rough-talking and mean when the occasion called for it.

During Joe's first week in Chicago, Blackburn refused to allow him to enter the ring. Instead, he made Joe work the big bag daily and punch out his frustration. "He'd hold the bag and give me instructions on how to throw punches," Joe recalls. "I did this morning, noon, and night till I could have sworn the bag was punching me, too."

When, at last, Blackburn allowed Joe to box for him, he saw the young fighter's faults immediately. Joe was hitting off-balance, a dangerous fault. A counter punch from an opponent could knock him down, put him out. Blackburn began to correct the fault by showing Joe how to plant his feet and punch with the full weight of his body, not just swinging his arms. "People who go to fights didn't want to see no dancer," he told Joe. "They want to see a man who goes for the guts. You got the strength to beat or knock out anybody you want to if you plant your body in the right position and use all that weight."

One day after training began, Blackburn said, "You know, boy, the heavyweight division for a Negro is hardly likely. The white man ain't too keen on it. You have to really be something to get anywhere. If you really ain't gonna be another Jack Johnson, you got some hope. White man hasn't forgotten that fool nigger with his white woman, acting like he owned the world. And you got to listen to everything I tell you. You got to jump when I say jump, sleep when I say sleep. Other than that, you're wasting your time and mine."

Joe gave Blackburn a serious look, promised his trainer and himself that there would be no time wasted.

"Okay, Chappie." Blackburn gave him a little, tight-lipped smile.

Joe smiled back, said, "Okay, Chappie."

It was another first for Joe: the first time in his life that he had adhered to so much routine. He ran six miles each morning at 6:00 a.m., twice around Washington Park. He punched the heavy bag, sparred and skipped rope. All the time Blackburn was there, telling him over and over and over again how to punch with the full weight of his body.

Joe took to laughing when Blackburn told him how black fighters were allowed into the ring just to make the white fighters look good. "They let you put up a good fight, but you dare not look better than some of the worst white boxers you supposed to be fighting."

It was better now than it had been in Blackburn's day, the trainer told the young Louis. He, Blackburn, who wore a size eight and a half shoe, used to slip into a size ten before each fight. He had made sure he got paid his gold pieces in advance, tucked them away in the over-sized shoes. That way, the promoters, again mostly white, could not skip out without paying.

"Sometime, someplace, one of them dudes is gonna try to get to you to throw a fight," the trainer told Joe. He stared the young fighter straight in the eye. "I done a lot of things I haven't been proud of but I never threw a fight, and you won't either 'cause I'll know, and then it's going to be you and me, Chappie. You an' me."

A few days before the night of the fight, the first professional bout, it was Chappie and Joe alone, Chappie giving him a rubdown. Chappie kept telling Joe how the odds were stacked against a black fighter opposing white fighters and the white promotional machine. "You can't win on points alone," he reit-erated sternly. "Negro fighters do not go to town win-ning decisions."

Joe nodded thoughtfully.

"It's real nice that you're so easygoing," Blackburn continued. "But you got to get some blood in your eyes. When you're in the ring, even with your sparring part-ners, you go for the kill. You let your right fist be the referee."

On July 4, 1934, Joe, Chappie, Black, Roxborough and Freddie Guinyard headed for the Bacon Casino on the South Side of Chicago. Because of his reputation in Golden Gloves, Joe had not had to fight preliminaries. This was to be a main event—something of a feather for a young fighter making his debut as a professional. He was to go against Jack Kracken out of Chicago, and the amount of rounds—ten instead of the three fought as an amateur—had Joe nervous. He wasn't sure he could go that far and told Chappie.

"Don't worry," Chappie reassured. "If you can go three, you can go six. If you can go six, you can go ten. Don't *worry*!"

It helped until Joe stepped through the ropes into the ring. He stared across the expanse of canvas at Jack Kracken. Kracken didn't look at all like the amateur fighters he had faced in the past. He was white and wearing white trunks, and looked older and much more experienced. He weighed in at 175. Joe had the edge there at 181. What bothered Joe most was the fact that Kracken didn't seem the least bit concerned about the black dude in the opposite corner. The white boy looked like he had it made, and that bothered Joe lots.

"Remember everything I taught you." Chappie could see he was nervous. "You get in there and knock that guy out as fast as you can. One clean punch is better than a hundred punches. Ride your time."

Joe looked again at Kracken. He was top honcho out of Chicago in the heavyweight division, and looked it. The bell sounded. Joe forgot everything except what Chappie had taught him.

Both fighters shuffled to center ring . . . Kracken arrogant, sure of himself. Joe went straight in for the body. When the white boxer dropped his guard, Joe him him with a strong left to the chin. It was the beginning of the end for Kracken. Joe Louis had knocked out his first professional opponent in less than two minutes of the first round. Like Chappie had said, no black fighter went to town on no decision in those days.

Joe and Freddie played the fool, jumping around like two idiots, hooting and hollering. Joe was proud of himself, but Chappie, Mr. Roxborough and Mr. Black didn't seem happy. Joe had appeared sluggish in the ring, was their combined opinion. There had to be a good reason for that, Chappie knew. He asked Joe about what he had been eating.

Joe became indignant. "I stuck to my diet," he complained, then frowned. " 'Cepting for the dozen bananas I ate before the fight."

Roxborough and Chappie and Black merely looked at him, shook their heads. It had seemed innocent enough at the time, but now, the three of them making him feel like the fool he had acted after the victory, Joe knew he had committed an unpardonable sin. After that, everybody watched every move he made before a fight.

Fifty-nine dollars. It was Joe's share of the purse. Joe could hardly believe he had earned that much for less than two minutes' work in the ring. Joe was learning a lot—about fighting from Chappie, and about life from Roxborough and the others in his camp. Black and Roxborough had a big investment in him, and they were not about to have that investment messed up through scandal. Not only was Joe in training as a fighter, but he had to live his personal life a certain way, too. Jack Johnson had all but ruined boxing for blacks, especially black heavyweights. There were no "written" rules. But there was day-to-day advice, especially about women. No one said, "Don't go out with girls, Joe." But they did impress the fact that if his picture were taken, as Jack Johnson's was so many times during his reign, it would be the end of Joe Louis' career.

Like any celebrity, people were watching Joe now, and would watch him even closer as his reputation grew. He was going to be a big man, sought after. Not all of those who sought him out would be friends. Chappie and Roxborough and Black compared it to the little black dolls made in the image of fighters. Those dolls always had a wide grin, and thick, very red lips. They were foolish-looking toys, almost obscene in the caricature they portrayed of the black man. Joe got the message: don't look like a fool nigger doll. Be a black man with dignity.

"Never go to a nightclub alone," they advised.

No big problem. Joe had never been to a nightclub alone or otherwise, he had no real desire to visit one.

"We got to maintain a good public image," they insisted.

Joe remembered what his momma had said about always leading a good Christain life. God, there was so much to learn and remember even outside the ring. He listened and tried to absorb, and tried to be worthy of so much good will. It seemed that he had barely turned round when he was staring his next fight in the face, this time against Willie Davis, a black fighter, in the same ring where he had put Kracken away.

July 11, 1934. Joe Louis by a knockout over Davis in the third round. He and Willie were friends. But in the ring there were no friendships, only winners and losers, and Davis was tough. There would be no "easy" fights, Joe was learning. This time his share of the purse was $62.

And then he fought Larry Udell on July 29, 1934 at the Marigold Gardens. An eight-rounder. The promoters were looking real hard at Joe Louis by now, speculating, and opened their eyes even more when he knocked Udell out in the second round. Winner's purse this time was $101. Joe was on top of the world, feeling good, looking fine.

The Louis-Udell fight ticket had been a sellout, and the Marigold gardens booked Joe again for August 13. Jack Kranz was to be his next opponent. He was a tough fighter, coming along the hard way, just as Joe was doing. It was a six-rounder, a decision. Joe took home the winner's purse of $125 on points.

"You're in a man's game now," Roxborough and Black repeatedly told Joe. There was no time to do more than take in an occasional movie, and train, train, train.

The rigid schedule began to pay off even more on August 27, 1934 when Joe knocked out Buck Everett in the second round. The winner's purse this time was $250. It was a sobering amount to a farm boy who had considered $60 a week big money. Joe began to realize just how much money there was to be made. He recalled Roxborough's beautiful home and attractive wife, the good things in life that he and Momma and the rest of the family had never experienced. The newspapers were beginning to talk about him, the purses were rapidly growing, and everything seemed right with the world.

It was time for the big kill, time to go back home and fight, Roxborough and Black decided. It was sort of a "local boy makes it big and returns" type scheme. The sports editors at the Detroit Times made arrangements for Joe to appear at the Naval Armory. The following from his amateur days at the Armory was still there, but this time he was coming in as a professional. Joe was not about to let the "home folks" down. He was to go against Alex Borchuk of Canada this time, a fighter with a reputation for being tough.

Suddenly Mr. Roxborough was summoned to the offices of the Michigan State Boxing Comission. When he arrived, Bingo Brown, the Commissioner, several white fight managers, and Eddie Edgar, the sports editor of the Detroit Free Press, were waiting. Bingo tried to convince Mr. Roxborough that it would be in everyone's best interest if he took on a white co-manager for Louis—things being as they were. Roxborough laughed, said, "No way, palsy. No way!"

"Well, then, your boy'll never again fight in Michigan,'' Bingo threatened.

Roxborough left the office without further comment. When he related the story to Joe, Black and Blackburn, he said, ''We'll take our chances. If that's the way they want it, then that's the way it'll have to be.''

In retrospect, the incident makes Joe even angrier than when it first happened. The white folks behind the Detroit boxing machine couldn't stand to see a black man on the rise. They wanted a piece of him free. But Roxborough held his ground and the gang—or whatever it is they called it back then—backed down. Had Roxborough relented, sold out under pressure, Joe Louis may never have reached the heights he attained, for it was common garden knowledge that the fight game thrived on boxers taking dives when the odds were right, and becoming, as so many black men before Joe had done, one of the red-lipped nigger dolls grinning for Mr. Charlie.

On the night of the fight, the Detroit police reserve had to be called out to handle the overflow crowd at the Armory. Joe's momma refused to attend. She knew he couldn't be whupped, but simply could not stand seeing her baby boy hit even once. Most of the rest of Joe's family was there, however. Bennie Mitchell, too. It gave Joe even more confidence. He knew he was going to do it, knew he had to.

It was a tougher fight than Joe had anticipated. Borchuk was a bull, much like the contemporary Canadian, George Chavallo. He hit so hard that he chipped one of Joe's back teeth, and by the end of the third round the young Bomber was feeling discouraged. ''Go in there and do like I taught you,'' Chappie kept saying between rounds. ''Work on his body till he drops dead. You got 'im, Chappie. You *got* 'im!''

Joe listened to Chappie. The bell rang for round four.

He thought he had hit Borchuk with everything he had, and that the Canadian was immune to his blows. But Chappie insisted that Joe just wasn't seeing straight out there under the hot lights. He had, in fact, gotten to him, the trainer instead. In round four, what Chappie said turned out to be true again: a knockout! The crowd went wild. Joe Louis was victorious again.

The purse was over $200 that night—Joe forgets the exact amount. The money was rolling in. Joe was the toast of Detroit, had earned the distinction. He celebrated by treating all of his friends and family to a night of bowling.

Within days of the Borchuk fight, Chicago was calling to get Joe back for a bout with Adolph Wiater. From Green Bay, Wisconsin, Wiater had beaten Johnny Risko, and Risko was an outstanding contender for the heavyweight crown. The fight was scheduled for September 25, 1934 at the Arcadia Gardens.

One day just before the fight, Joe walked into the gym to see Chappie standing there with a brick in his hand. Joe stopped. Chappie raised his arm as if about to fling the brick. Natural reflex: Joe ducked. "See what I'm trying to teach you?" Chappie said. "Pretend you have a brick in your fist. Naturally the guy's gonna duck, then you hit him with the other hand."

It was simple enough for Joe to understand. Chappie's advice was always like that—garden variety. Joe tried to put the new idea into motion on the night of the Wiater fight, but Wiater was tough. He was the first man to bring blood to Joe's face. A crowder, an inside fighter, he took the young Bomber the route but lost it on the decision. Joe came away from the ring hurt some and $300 richer.

Next lesson at the gym next day was how to deal with a crowder. "Catch 'im under the arm, spin 'im around and bang him in the jaw,'' Chappie said and demonstrated. Joe caught on quick. Nobody crowded him much after that.

Art Sykes of New York came next, October 24. It was a hard bout for Joe. Sykes was full of heart, and pretty good. Joe got to him in the eighth with a powerful right to the jaw. Sykes was out. He had to be dragged to his corner as if drugged, nor could his seconds revive him. The physicians were called in. Nothing. Joe began to sweat. Had he killed the man? No, that could not be—please, God. If he had killed a man in the ring he would give up boxing, he silently promised. Please, God, don't let Art Sykes die.

A few hours later word got back to Joe that Sykes was recovering at the hospital. He was feeling good, feeling fine again, and with a $450 purse. That was *big* money in the 30s, and Joe was training so much and fighting so often that he had no chance to spend what he made. He sent money home—no more welfare, no more worrying about simple things like food and rent and clothing. The Barrows were bursting with pride over the hardheaded youngster who had, in spite of it all, gotten up there with the big guys.

But it was only a beginning, Joe knew. Now he was convinced of his ability, of the knowledge Roxborough and Blackburn and Black had passed along. So much lay ahead, so much behind. The red clay hills of Alabama were behind him forever, no more dirt poor, hungry days, and stomach-growling nights. No sir, not for Joe. Not as long as he knew how to punch, listened to Chappie. He would never end up a Jack Johnson or a red-lipped nigger doll, not Jolting Joe. There were other hazards he could not begin to imagine, including the government and a periodically scrambled brain. But in 1934, still young and on top of the world, there seemed

to be nothing but success and wealth on the horizon.
Young Joe Louis was feeling good, looking fine.

The Joe Louis-Max Schmeling fight of June 19,
1936, captured the attention of everyone in the
boxing world, including that of former
heavyweight great Jack Dempsey.

June 22, 1938: At Yankee Stadium, Joe Louis shakes the hand of Max Schmeling, the same hand that put him to sleep when they fought at the same sight almost exactly two years earlier.

6

One wonders what course of action the nineteen-year-old Louis would have taken if he had somehow been allowed to peer into the future and see himself thirty-six years later on May 1, 1970. There was no inkling yet, nothing to even hint at the tragic events to come. Nineteen-seventy was a long, long way ahead. But on that morning, a Friday, one could not help but wonder if Jolting Joe would have continued in his boxing career if he could have heard Martha Lewis—not yet his wife in 1934—caution the Denver Sheriff's Department, "Come in the back way, through the garage that leads into the kitchen. That way, nobody will see you. There'll be no fuss."

No fuss! Martha had arranged to spend that particular Friday, May 1, 1970, at the home of a cousin. Neither of Joe's children would be there either. Both his daughter and son, like Martha, had made arrangements to be elsewhere.

Martha had made arrangements for the Reverend Carl Walker to stay with Joe. As a divinity student, the minister had lived with the Lewis' and felt at home at their place. Moreover, Joe accepted the minister's presence without suspicion or resentment. It seemed he was suspicious of everyone these days, and resentful of most things. Yet everyone knew there was something desperately wrong with Joe.

It had been a busy week for Martha. Having coaxed Joe to Denver in the hope he would find some relief for his anxieties in pleasant, familiar surroundings, their home, her hopes were shattered the first night. Joe, alone in his bedroom, literally tore a lamp apart. It was a telltale sign. Something desperate had to be done to counteract the desperate thing happening to Joe.

Worst of all, Joe did not think he was sick. Martha visited Dr. John H. MacDonald, chief of forensic psychiatry at Colorado General Hospital, quickly outlined the tragic situation. A lengthy discussion of Joe's illness followed. "Joe still doesn't believe he's sick," Martha told the doctor, whose reputation she'd known long before she decided to come to Colorado. "It's going to be impossible to get him to come here to see you." She paused, nervous. What she had to do was not easy. "Would . . . would it be possible to have you come to our house for consultation?" she blurted at last.

The arrangements for the in-home consultation were made. Mrs. Louis then went to see Stephen L.R. Mc-Nichols, one-time governor of Colorado. McNichols was an old friend. Martha felt that Joe would be less apprehensive if McNichols was present when Dr. Mac-Donald arrived.

The group gathered in the living room of the Louis home. Joe sat placedly on a Louis XV couch set against a long wall, directly below a picture of him in his classic boxing pose. The man beneath the picture was a mere caricature of his former self. Time had worked harshly on Joe. He was balding. His eyes, once so steady, so firmly on target in the ring, now darted apprehensively in a jowl-hung face. McNichols and MacDonald confronted him from across the room.

Within minutes, pleasant greetings deteriorated into suspiciousness, and the probing examination by Dr. MacDonald . Joe began to trace his labyrinthian delusions. His position was adamantly against a program of psychiatric solution. The confrontation lasted forty-five minutes; then, curtly, McNichols and Dr. MacDonald left.

"Joe is a very sick man," was Dr. MacDonald's analysis afterward. He advised Martha to act with haste. "For your own sake as well as Joe's."

Under Colorado law, it was possible, upon verification by a qualified physician, to obtain from the probate court an order to hospitalize, for a period of up to three months, person deemed in need of psychiatric treatment. Armed with a letter from Dr. MacDonald, Martha petitioned for the court order that would commit Joe to the Colorado Psychiatric Hospital "for observation, diagnosis, and treatment for mental illness for a period not to exceed three months unless extended by further order of the court." Martha, Punchy and Jacqueline, Joe's children, signed the application designed to commit Joe.

The application was presented to Judge David Brofman of the probate court. Attached were letters from

Dr. MacDonald, and Drs. Robert C. Bennett and James Ellison, both of Detroit. In chambers, Judge Brofman signed the order to hospitalize the former heavyweight champion of the world.

The court order directed "the sheriff of the City and County of Denver to pick up the respondent at 2675 Monaco Parkway or wherever he may be found in the City and County of Denver and deliver respondent to Colorado Psychiatric Hospital, *forthwith.*"

Louis was home when the Sheriff's Department vehicle arrived in the driveway at the back of the house. Reverend Walker had been prepared for the visitors. Three uniformed deputy sheriffs and Mose Trujillo, a liaison officer with the probate court, stepped quietly in. "He's in the front part of the house," Walker explained. "I'll tell him you're here."

The officers waited in the kitchen at the back of the house. They shuffled apprehensively, each no doubt wondering how the former heavyweight champion would react to their presence and the court order.

Louis appeared. He was obviously distressed. He confronted Trujillo. "I won't leave unless you let me call the White House first. I know Nixon. I want to tell the President what you are doing to me."

Without objection from the officers, Joe went to the telephone and put through a call to Washington, D.C. When he asked for Nixon, he was told that he could talk to a White House aide but not the president.

"Okay, then I got to call all the newspapers and radio and TV and stations," Joe told the officers. "I want everybody to know what you are doing to me."

Confusion. A bending of the once great champion's desires, disregard for his wishes. Joe put through calls to the *Denver Post* and the *Rocky Mountain News.* Soon, cameramen and reporters began to pour into the

Louis living room. Abruptly, two other newcomers appeared: someone had summoned Irving P. Andrews, Louis' attorney in Denver, and Truman Coles, the public defender. Coles acted quickly, advised Louis not to talk to reporters. Then, aware that Louis was under legal restraint, Andrews advised his client to prepare himself for the trip to Colorado Psychiatric Hospital.

Joe paused for a long moment, lost in his own thoughts. The officers glanced from the obviously distraught former champion to the picture of him above the Louis XV couch on the living room wall. Was this the same man? What had happened in the thirty-odd years since Joe Louis began his professional career as a boxer to bring about this? It was a question millions of concerned Americans would ask themselves when the story broke in the papers across the country next day . . . *why was this was happening to one of the greatest heavyweight champions the world had ever known?*

Joe packed a small leather bag of personal belongings while the sheriff's officers watched. Their guns were holstered but the three were visibly nervous. They, too, it seemed, remembered Joe as the fearsome Brown Bomber. Anything could happen, they obviously supposed.

Having packed his bag, Joe donned a topcoat over his tan pants and white shirt. He paused again, then went to the refrigerator for an apple. He bit hard into the fruit, munched. The powerful jaw that had shook off so many brutal punches worked speculatively. He nodded to the sheriff's officers. Unrestrained, the once mighty Louis left through the back way of his own house, through the garage, and stepped quietly into the deputy sheriff's car. The doors of the car slammed, shattering the silence and jarring the nerves of those who stood watching.

No one would have guessed such in 1934.

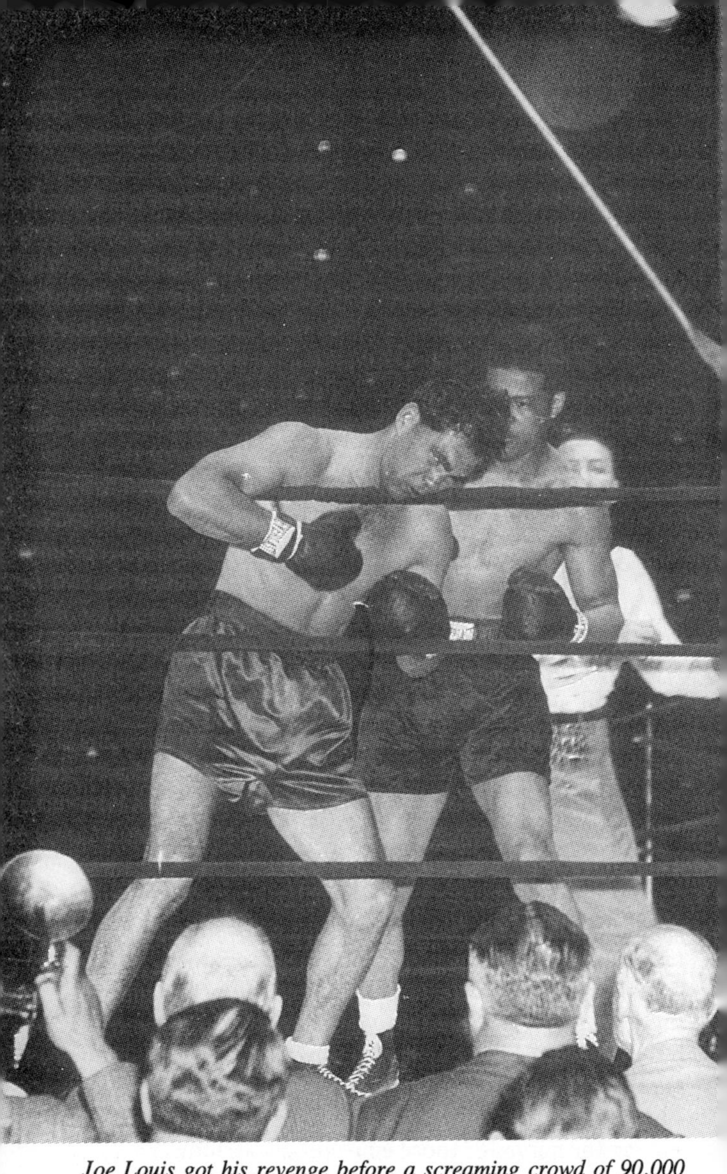

Joe Louis got his revenge before a screaming crowd of 90,000 fans at Yankee Stadium. The pride of Nazi Germany and former world champion was knocked out in the first round.

7

In Chicago, back in 1934 after the Art Sykes fight, Roxborough and Black told the young Joe Louis that his name was becoming famous all over the country, but that a lot of promoters were saying he was facing easy opponents, the bouts arranged by his managers to make him look good. It was time for Joe to fight a nationally known heavyweight, one whose ability could not be questioned by the promoters or the public. And the bout would have to be scheduled for a big arena—Madison Square Garden. Joe had to prove once and for all that he was the real thing.

The opponent was found, Stanley Poreda, the heavyweight champion of Hoboken, New Jersey. Poreda was a hot name in the East. He also had a "national" reputation. The bout was scheduled for the Arcadia Gardens, Chicago, on November 14. It was a major step up. Joe knew he had to beat Poreda.

Ironically, the Poreda fight turned out to be one of the easiest matches of Joe's career; knockout, round one. Still there were doubts. Many promoters and journalists asked, "Could he do it again?" They came up with the next toughest fighter they could find. It was Charley Massera of Monongahela, Pennsylvania this time. He was known as the "knockout artist." All the eastern papers were raving about him.

November 30, Chicago Stadium: Joe Louis by a knockout over Charley Massera in the third round. Joe's share of the purse was $1,200. The fight business was good to Joe and getting better all the time.

Joe recalls, again ironically, "The first time I ever broke training was in Chicago before the Massera fight."

One of the ladies in the building where Joe was living had a daughter who was much older than Joe. Ten days before the Massera fight, the woman talked Joe into going to bed with her. Next morning when Joe went out to do roadwork he felt so guilty about the incident that he ran ten miles instead of the proscribed five. It was obviously Momma's influence: *always lead a good clean Christian life*. Joe just ran and ran. Then, instead of boxing three rounds, he went six. "What the hell is wrong with you?" Chappie Blackburn wanted to know.

"I feel good," Joe lied. He couldn't tell Chappie. There he was, supposedly in training for a big fight, and fooling around with some woman.

But the incident had not affected Joe's ability to knock out Massera, and now there was less talk about Roxborough and Blackburn arranging fights with *easy* opponents.

Bowling, golf and baseball games had always been Joe's major recreational pastimes. In later years, golf would reign foremost, but during the early stages of his career, while coming up, he followed the ball clubs avidly. Joe loved the game. He still harbored a childhood desire to be a baseball player, and one day, shortly after the Massera fight, he recalls mentioning it to his friend, Holman Williams.

"You don't want to do that," Holman countered. "A colored ball player has the cards stacked against him and he can't even get merchandise checks. At least at fighting you might make a few bucks."

It was before the days of Civil Rights movements and Supreme Court decisions that allowed black folks to dream. Besides, boxing was the only thing Joe knew. He shrugged off the idea of becoming a ball player, concentrated again on the thing he did best of all.

Lee Ramage of Los Angeles was to be Joe's last fight in 1934. Ramage was considered as tough as—if not tougher than—Louis. He had never been knocked out, and the promoters were anxious to pit the two. Mr. Black saw the potential, held out until Chicago Stadium offered Joe $2,750 to go against Ramage in their arena. It was to be a big fight, important to Joe's career. There would be no more incidents to break training like the girl in the hotel, he promised himself.

But while Joe was training in the Chicago gym, something even more significant was to happen to him. Lots of people came to watch the young heavyweight beat the bag and his sparring partners. Among them, one day— Joe barely saw her out of the corner of one eye—was the most beautiful girl he had ever laid eyes on. She was five-foot-six, pretty hair, pretty complexion and exuded class. She had come to the gym because an insurance executive friend of hers had promised to introduce her to the next Heavyweight Champion of the World, but left before Joe could meet her.

Shortly thereafter, Joe sat for an interview with sportswriter, Al Monroe, at the Chicago Defender. The beautiful girl from the gym was still on his mind—a vision. Marva Trotter. Coincidentally, she was working as a secretary at the Defender. Now he knew her name and where to find her. But the Ramage fight held priority over everything else.

The sportswriters had been right about Lee Ramage, Joe learned on December 14. He was smart, a scientist in the ring. He knew boxing, danced away from Joe's killer punches. There was only one way to get to him, Joe decided: corner him. Get him where he could not get away.

Joe's chance came in the third round. Maneuvering Ramage into a corner, he hit the boxer with a hard left to the body, followed by a brutal right to the jaw. Ramage sagged, went down slowly. Another knockout for Louis. He had finished his first year as a professional. His record stood at twelve fights, all wins. Ten of those victories had been through knockouts, and two by decision. It called for a celebration.

"Chappie," Joe said after the Ramage fight. "I'm having a party and I want you to invite that girl Marva that came to visit the gym."

Chappie gave Joe a knowing look, and complied. Marva came to the party at the Grand Hotel in Chicago, along with her sister, Gladys. While the party went on around them, Joe and Marva sat and talked about the things they each wanted to do in life. Marva was attending the Vogue School t f Designing in Chicago and had aspirations toward being a great designer. She was also taking part-time courses in English at the University of Chicago and working as a stenographer. She was only eighteen, but the first really ambitious woman Joe had ever met.

When the evening ended, it was agreed that they could see each other again when Joe got back from Detroit. It was Christmas time, time to be with the family—Momma Barrow and Poppa Brooks, and all those brothers and sisters. It was, in many respects, the best Christmas the family had ever had. Money flowed freely, didn't mean a thing to Joe except the happiness it could bring those he loved. He was happy and the family was happy.

He thought lots about Marva—eighteen and so beautiful and ambitious. She was a real lady. She had been born in Muskogee, Oklahoma, she had told him at the party, and had moved with her family to Chicago when she was five. It was hard to believe that she had so much going for her, was so different from the other girls he knew. Even Bennie. Bennie could not hold a candle to Marva Trotter, he decided, no way. It was almost too good to be true that they had met, and that he had a tentative date with her when he returned to Chicago. There was much to celebrate this Christmas, much to give thanks for, and even more to look for in '35.

It was about time to relax and enjoy. Wealth and fame were merely a whisper away, Joe was certain now. His next bout? There would be no doubt in the minds of promoters and sportswriters this time, no question about his ability. He recalled what the insurance agent had told Marva Trotter when he invited her to the gym to watch the workout: "I'm gonna introduce you to the next Heavyweight Champion of the World."

At one time it had seemed far-fetched. Now? Now, May 1, 1970 was a long ways away.

After winning the heavyweight title by beating James Braddock on June 22, 1937, Joe Louis became one of the most popular men in the world—with the exception of Germany.

8

Indeed, the new year was to be a big one for Joe. Roxborough had decided that Joe was ready for New York. A call was put through to James J. Johnson, the boxing promoter at Madison Square Garden. Johnson said, "You're a colored manager and so's your fighter. You're going to make the same money as the white boys and your boy is going to have to lose a few." In the end, the deal was turned down because Johnson didn't feel that colored fighters would be a box office draw, and he would be taking a risk.

Chappie laughed after the telephone conversation. Before calling Johnson, Roxborough had asked Chappie if he thought Joe was ready for New York. "Sure, he's ready for New York, but New York ain't ready for him," Chappie had answered. Now both Roxborough and Joe knew what he had been talking about.

On January 4, Joe went against Patsy Perroni from Cleveland. It was a scheduled ten-rounder at the Detroit Olympic Arena. Patsy was a tough, persistent fighter. Joe knocked him down three times during the match, but he always managed to come back up off the canvas. His counter punches staggered Joe several times throughout the bout, but the decision went to Louis. Joe's purse? Four thousand dollars! And now observers knew that he could take it as well as dish it out.

Hans Birkie came next. The Duquesne Garden in Pittsburg, January 11. Joe was heavier now, tipping in at 194. Birkie fought a courageous fight, but Louis knocked him out in the tenth. Joe's share of the purse was $1,900.

Roxborough was still trying for New York, grumbling about wasted talent and not getting top dollar. Joe paid little attention . . . $6,000 in seven days was more money than he had once thought existed in the world. True, he had not yet made Madison Square Garden, the epitome of success in the fight game. but Lee Ramage was asking for a return match and things were moving fast enough for Joe. The rematch was set for February 11 in Los Angeles, California.

Joe took a few days to get back to Chicago to see Marva. It was a sweet reunion: Marva introduced him to her parents, seven sisters and three brothers. Then she introduced him around to her friends. It was nice to be able to take her out without having to sneak around as he had done with Bennie in Detroit. People recognized him in Chicago and crowded around wherever he took the girl. It was a new and pleasant experience, and he liked Marva even more than he originally thought. He was proud to be seen with her, and she with him.

In the rematch with Ramage, Joe knocked him out with a strong left to the jaw in round two. People had said he should not fight Ramage at Los Angeles, the other man's homeground. He, Joe, would not get a fair shake if it went to a decision, people had said. But there was nothing no one could do about giving other than a fair shake on a knockout, and the purse, again, was a bit over $4,000.

The papers were having a heyday. It seemed there was nothing anyone could do to keep Joe from winning. Newsmen began to come up with names like *Dark Destroyer* and the *Alabama Assassin*. Other would be nicknames included the *Detroit Destroyer, Michigan Mauler, Sepia Socker,* and . . . the *Brown Bomber*. Somehow the latter stuck. It would be with Joe for the rest of his career.

The name stuck, and suddenly there were a lot of black people around wanting to pump Joe's hand. He was their savior, they claimed. "Show them whites," some shouted. "Brown Bomber, Brown Bomber!"

Joe was still the simple farm boy at heart, not sophisticated enough to understand that he was a symbol. No one since Jack Johnson had done what he was doing, no black man. But Johnson had degraded the black image, where Louis, in his personal lifestyle and ring ethics, was building it stronger and stronger with each successive fight. Little did either Joe or his fans suspect that image would be put to the supreme test by Nazi Germany in only a few short years.

The next bout was a pushover, and Joe knew it. His opponent's name this time was Donald "Reds" Barry. Joe could have put the man away any time in the match, but he had met a San Francisco sportswriter, Harry Smith, whom he liked, and had told Smith he would put Barry out in the third. Smith printed the story as his own prediction, and Joe, not wanting to disappoint a friend, had carried Barry through the first two rounds.

The next bout was scheduled for March 28 in Detroit. Natie Brown, a tough boy to go against. It was while in training for this fight that Joe met Nat Fleisher, sportswriter and owner of *Ring Magazine*. Fleisher loved heavyweights. He had been following Joe's career since the Brown Bomber turned pro. Fortunately for Joe, one of Fleisher's best friends was Mike Jacobs who had just organized the Twentieth Century Sporting Club and was going after the promoters who controlled Madison Square Garden—those who had turned down Roxborough's offer because they saw blacks as second class citizens. Mike felt that no one organization should have control of everything, especially heavyweights, where the real money was. Mike had the support of the William Randolph Hearst sportswriters, and the Hearst Milk Fund staged fights at Madison Square Garden for the purpose of obtaining milk for poor kids. The promoters at the Garden kept raising the rent whenever the Hearst Fund had an affair. A fatal mistake on the part of the promoters: most of the gate from the Hearst Fund affairs went to charity, and the Hearst people were pissed.

Mike Jacobs approached the Hearst people with his scheme. He told them if they would support his opposing club, he would not only charge the Fund less rent, but he would give a portion of the gate to the organization. It was a daring risk. But the top Hearst sportswriters all over the country liked Mike, and many of them considered him their friend.

They came in from New York the night after Joe beat Donald "Reds" Barry. Mike Jacobs told Roxborough about the newly formed heavyweight champion, Primo Carnera. Mike said he was coming out to Detroit to see the Natie Brown match and had reserved a car on the train to bring along a lot of East Coast sportsswriters. Roxborough almost jumped out of his pants for joy.

Joe was determined to make a good impression in the Natie Brown fight. But he was nervous, overanxious. Brown was what was known as a "spoiler." He did his best to show Joe up, and the Brown Bomber could barely get through the man's guard to land punches. Although Joe knocked him down in the first round, Brown managed to go the distance. He was the type of fighter with such a clumsy, awkward style that even the best looked bad in the same ring. Joe won the ten-round decision but was not at all happy about the fight.

They met Jacobs at a colored nightclub, the Frog Club, after the fight. Roxborough and Black and Chappie sat by quietly while Joe apologized for having looked so bad against Brown. Jacobs dismissed the apology. Then he told Joe that there was a sort of a silent agreement between promoters that there would never again be another black heavyweight champion the likes of Jack Johnson. He told Joe how Jack Dempsey had run all over the country to avoid fighting Harry Wills, a black fighter. And now Jacobs wanted *him*, Joe Louis, to go against Primo Carnera.

"If you can fight," Jacobs said, "I'll get you a shot at the title. "And I'll make a lot of money for you."

Amidst the noise of Joe's victory party, there was a long moment of silence at the table where Joe and the others sat. Finally, Roxborough said, "How you feel about the offer, Joe?" Black and Chappie wanted to know how he felt, too.

"You're my managers," Joe told them. "Whatever you say is fine with me."

Everyone in the group smiled, including Chappie. Then they all got up and went to the men's room to sign the contracts where it was quiet. The contract stipulated that Mike Jacobs would be the sole promoter for Louis' fights for the next three years, and with a renewal option for the end of the period. Over the years, some have tended to get the arrangement mixed up—like a *Who's-Who* in musical chairs. Mike Jacobs was the promoter, Roxborough and Black were Joe's managers, and Chappie was trainer. That's the way it began and the way it stayed. The big time, the *real* big time, Madison Square Garden, was just around the corner for the simple farm boy from the red clay hills of Alabama.

The move scared a lot of white folks in the fight game. Many began to search for worthy white opponents to stop Joe. They covered the world looking for a "white hope" to stop the Brown Bomber even before he got started. Joe himself was just beginning to realize how important the contract with Mike Jacobs was. Jacobs actually wanted him to be the world's next heavyweight champion.

Jacobs told Roxborough and Black that he would arrange for an advance while they set up a string of fights to keep Joe in the public eye until the Carnera match could be set. Joe's managers agreed to set up the fights but turned down the advance. That shocked Jacobs. That had always been one of the biggest problems with black or poor white managers . . . they got trapped into taking a promoter's money, and then had to fight—or dive—the way the man told them to. Not Joe. Not Roxborough or Black. And definitely not Chappie. Mike Jacobs was not interested in fixing fights, that was small time compared to what he could make with Joe as heavyweight champion and under exclusive contract with him. By holding out on the offered advance, Joe's managers demanded and got 37½ percent of the gate instead of the usual 12½ percent. Everything seemed to be going right for Joe now.

The string of matches leading up to the Carnera fight was set up to keep Joe in the public eye. The first was with Roy Lazer of Chicago on April 12: a knockout, round three. The third round seemed to be Joe's favorite—like a lucky charm each time that particular bell sounded. The gate from the Lazer fight ran $42,000. Nobody had expected that big of a draw. Nobody, including Joe's managers, realized just how many fight fans were coming out to see the Brown Bomber in action. Had Roxborough and Black guessed as much, they might have demanded a percentage of the gate rather than the guaranteed $10,000. But it would never happen again, they agreed after that one.

On April 22, Joe fought Biff Benton in Dayton, Ohio: knockout in the second round.

Roscoe Toles came next. The match was held in Flint, Michigan on April 27: knockout in the sixth.

Next Joe knocked out Willie Davis in Peoria, Illinois on May 3. Then Gene Stanton in Kalamazoo, Michigan on May 7, and another third round knockout. Joe was really feeling good, and looking real, real fine.

They were storming the country with knockouts, one right after the other. Now, there was hardly anyone who had not heard of Joe Louis. There was no time for anything except training, traveling to the next fight and whupping opponents. Joe somehow managed to sneak enough time in to buy a house for his mother and surprise her with it on Easter Sunday, 1935. This was what it was all about, what Joe had dreamed of. He was proud of having bought the house for Momma than of anything he had ever done. Soon afterward, he bought her a chicken ranch on the outskirts of Detroit, all paid for cash—no bills and lots more coming where that pile had come from. It was almost un-Christian to be able to make so much money.

It was about this time that Joe introduced Marva Trotter to his family. He had never before brought a girl home, had always realized that when he did she would have to be something special. Marva met him in Detroit with her sister—shoot! Joe was beginning to get the idea that he might have to marry the girl to ever get her off alone. Once he thought about it, it did not seem like such a very bad idea, especially when Momma and Marva began to act like mother and daughter.

The Primo Carnera fight was scheduled for June 25, 1935, at Yankee Stadium, New York City. Joe was confident. Carnera had won the championship from Jack Sharkey and had defended his title only twice before he was defeated by Max Baer in 1934. Chappie claimed that there had always been lots of doubt in fight circles about Carnera's ability, but that he was the gateway to the heavyweight championship for Joe.

The Louis entourage left Detroit in mid-May. Jacobs picked them up at the depot, took them straight to his office for a press conference. The conference rattled Joe some. There were too many cameras flashing, too many reporters and newsreels running. Joe simply could not answer questions as fast as the reports threw them his way.

When it was over, Joe breathed a sigh of relief, and he and Roxborough and Black and Chappie and Bill Bottoms got the hell out of there. It was a chance to see New York City, especially Harlem. Back home in Detroit folks talked about Harlem like the streets were made of precious stones or something. Joe settled back in the car that took them through Central Park, and felt exhilarated when they reached Seventh Avenue. Harlem looked like any other big city he'd seen, but it was

Harlem: a black cultural happening.

There was time before training camp. Time. Something Joe had had little of in the past year. He decided to use it to find out exactly what black people meant when they spoke the word "Harlem." First, for promotional purposes—always keep 'im in the public eye—Mr. Roxborough and Black had him booked at the Harlem Opera House where he did a boxing skit with Dusty Flecher, a well-known black comedian. Then Joe skipped rope and punched the speed bag while the band played *Anchors Aweigh.* And finally, Joe punched the bag out into the audience. Four shows daily. Between that and impulsive jaunts around town, Joe began to get the feel of the real meaning of Harlem: the laughter and gaiety that was a black way of life even in poverty, as well as the tragic glimpses of heart-felt despair. Harlem was a city like any other city, and yet a complete and separate entity unto itself, like the Brown Bomber.

Harlem was a black man's city, and Joe was a black man's man. Both stood apart and remained something special when verbalized.

It bothered Joe when he learned that the Negro press could not get ringside tickets like the rest of the press. Prejudice? He was beginning to understand better the true meaning of the word now. The promoters couldn't very well come right out and say they didn't want niggers in the press section, no way. Instead, they did it politely: "Sorry, no ringside tickets for the weekly press. That automatically eliminated all of the Negro press because black people couldn't afford to support a daily newspaper. Negro papers never made any money anyway because the stores and the people who manufactured consumer items didn't try to advertise to the Negro market. It was a liberal education for a simple farm boy. It made Joe angry. The way he figured it, black folks went to the store to buy their clothes and whatever else they needed just like everyone else, and the way the promoters and merchants were treating the Negro press was unfair. It upset Joe so much that he went to Mike Jacobs about it. It was something Joe had never thought about before, and something Mike Jacobs had never thought about either. That was the big trouble, Joe decided: nobody ever thought about the other little guy.

Suddenly it became an issue. Hype Igoe, a white writer for the *Journal American*, went to bat for the Negro writers. It brought results. The promoters decided to set up an auxiliary press. Joe felt good about having taken part in the maneuver. Now guys like Billy Rowe and Chester Washington of the *Pittsburg Courier*, Al Monroe of the *Chicago Defender*, and Rowan Dougherty of the *Amsterdam News* got their chance to be a little further up front where they could report the upcoming fight to the Negro papers.

Craziness. New York was full of it. Like the Cotton Club on 140th Street and Lenox Avenue. Right in the middle of Harlem, yet black people were not allowed in. White folks only. The club featured black entertainment and some of the more gorgeous black women to be found anywhere. Entertainers like Duke Ellington, Cab Calloway and Claude Hopkins appeared there, but *no niggers allowed.*

And girls. New York was full of beautiful black girls, and Joe was meeting a few, as well as celebrities. Like Bill "Bojangles" Robinson, the dancer, who introduced him to Marion Eggberg. She was a chorus girl at the Memo Club on 133rd Street and Seventh Avenue, and the most beautiful woman Joe had ever seen. Afterward, Joe saw her for years—she would meet him all over the country when he was fighting. Joe had also met Owney Madden, owner of the Cotton Club, who brought three girls to Joe's place one night after the club closed. One was Edna Mae Holly who would later become Sugar Ray Robinson's first wife. One of the other girls was Lena Horne. Madden said, "Take your pick, Joe."

Joe chose Lena. It was not all good Christian living out there on the road.

Then it was Pompton Lakes, New Jersey and important matters. Joe knew he had to excel in the Carnera fight and was determined to train harder than ever before. Carnera was a giant—his one asset. He was so big that he had tired many opponents simply by having them deal with his bulk. In preparation for the match, Chapie found the biggest guys he could as sparring partners. Joe kind of liked that. He had always felt that bigger guys gave him a bigger target to punch.

The entourage had set up camp in an old colonial house with several cottages around it on the border of the lake. It was pleasant and peaceful. The owner, a Dr. Joseph Bier, had converted an old barn into a bar, and hundreds of people came up daily to drink and watch Joe work out.

It was at the Pompton Lakes camp that Joe first met Jack Johnson, the last black heavyweight champion of the world. In spite of all he had heard about the man, Joe liked Johnson. "You going to run into every kind of situation possible," Johnson told the young fighter. "Keep your head at all times."

The grueling routine got underway: up at six to run at least five miles before breakfast, then eat a hunk of cheese, drink some fruit juice, take a shower and nap. Up again for a huge breakfast of oatmeal, half a dozen eggs, ham steaks, bread and milk. Dinner usually consisted of a three-pound steak and salad. Bill Bottoms would always see to it that Joe got a dish of black-eyed peas when he wanted, and supplied the quart of ice cream the Bomber ate almost every night.

Lots of noise was being made about the Carnera fight. Trouble had begun in Europe with Mussolini already threatening Ethiopia. Carnera was Italian, Joe was black, and the whole world was looking on. Several black groups even came to the Pompton Lakes Camp to tell Joe he represented Ethiopia. Some talked to the Brown Bomber about Marcus Garvey. Joe had never even heard Garvey's name, never mind his plan to ship all the black folks in America back to Africa. It was heavy. Almost too heavy for Joe's twenty-year-old shoulders.

Even the Hearst people were getting nervous about the Italian-Ethiopian business and considered cancelling the fight. Fortunately, Roxborough talked them out of it, and Joe promised to contribute ten percent of his purse to the Milk Fund. This one had to be fought, Joe knew. It had to be fought and won because Joe wanted to go against Max Baer next. He had watched Baer fight against Jimmy Braddock on June 13 and was not impressed by the man: Baer kept swinging at Braddock and missing him throughout the bout, and Braddock had won the championship. "Hell, I'm ready for that kind of fight right now," Joe had grumbled to Chappie and his managers, who told him he was still young and black and had to wait his turn. That turn would come soon, he knew . . . just so long as the Carnera fight went off on schedule and he could beat the white lummox.

They broke camp two days before the fight, returned to Harlem where Joe was to rest up. But every place he went in New York City became a madhouse, people waiting to get close, pump his hand and reassure him about the Carnera fight. The weigh-in at the State Office Building was almost a riot. Mounted policemen had to clear a path for Joe and Carnera to enter. Joe got his first closeup look at the "Italian hope." He was indeed huge: six-foot-five-and-three-quarters and 260 1½ pounds. Joe was impressed but not intimidated. Carnera kept making faces at him, making dumb comments . . . like the nigger dolls with big red lips, only Carnera wasn't a nigger to speak of.

Then the night of the fight Joe was awestruck by the size of the crowd. He had never seen so many people in one place in his life: sixty thousand crowding Yankee Stadium ball park. Reputedly, it was the largest number of people to attend a fight in New York City since 1927. And, in Joe's mind, they were all out there waiting to see him beat up on this funny-face giant who was a moose in comparison.

Chappie kept talking to Joe, rubbing his back and drilling in tactics. "Work his body till he drops his guard," Chappie said. "Then headhunt. Go for his head. But work on that body first, Chappie. Make them big arms drop down."

In retrospect, Joe admits to having been nervous. But he was always nervous when he first stepped into the ring—no big thing. It was the adrenalin flowing, preparing his body for battle against Goliath. The referee called them to center ring, gave instructions. Then Joe was back in his corner waiting for the bell for round one to ring. Nervous still . . . this was *really* the big one. He knew the jitteriness would disappear once he landed the first punch to Carnera. The nervousness had more to do with waiting for that first bell than anything else. When it sounded, he was up, shuffling forward toward the hulk who was still grinning like one of those big-lipped nigger dolls.

Following Chappie's instructions, Joe landed several hard punches in round one. Carnera seemed helpless, merely flicking jabs at the Brown Bomber. It seemed to shock the Italian, as well as the spectator audience, that Joe was handling him like a baby instead of it being the other way around. Everyone had been looking at Carnera's size, not his talent.

In the fifth round, they clinched, and Joe picked Carnera up off his feet. The huge Italian spoke for the first time during the fight, said, "Oh . . . oh." His eyes bulged in surprise. "I should be doing this to you," he added in dismay.

Joe was almost as surprised as Carnera at the ease with which he moved the big man around. The Italian had nothing going for him except bulk, it seemed. He had a jab but no punch. Instead, he *pushed* with his right. It was an awkward style, if style it could be called. Mostly the big man tried to intimidate Joe with his superior weight.

Joe was finding it hard to get under Carnera's guard, however. Chappie had told him to pace himself, watch. The openings would come, Chappie had insisted.

Moments before the bell ending round six rang, Chappie yelled, "Go get him."

It was like a programmed reflex. Joe obeyed, hit Carnera with a telling right. Blood spurted from the Italian's mouth. Then Joe knocked him down for the first time with a right to the jaw. Then he knocked him down again with *another* right to the jaw. Then he finished the giant off with a left-right combination. The Italian went down for the third time and last time and just lay there. So much for Mussolini and Ethiopia.

Joe was exuberant, bouncing around his corner along

with Chappie. Carnera had not hurt him even once. He was loaded for bear—spelled *Max Baer!* Or Jimmy Braddock or anyone. There was no more question about Joe Louis' boxing ability. He had made it in New York, the boxing capital of the world. He had $60,000 as his share of the purse to prove it.

There was much speculation about where Joe would fight next. Some cities were offering their stadiums free. Roxborough and Black convinced Mike Jacobs that the next match should take place in the city where Joe had started his professional career—Chicago. Harry "Kingfish" Levinsky looked like the best prospect, they decided. He had a reputation as a strong hitter, and Joe would be able to prove the one thing he didn't show in the Carnera fight. Mainly, that he could take as well as dish out the punishment. It all amazed Joe . . . the way his managers figured it all out. It was like putting the pieces of a jigsaw puzzle together. When it was done, when the pieces all fit, the finished puzzle would be the heavyweight championship crown.

Joe was somewhat disappointed that Baer would not be next. He was learning, however. He was learning that he was a black man in a predominantly white man's profession, and that he had to bide his time for the rest of the good things to come.

If he ever got overanxious, Chappie was there in his corner to steer him the right way.

By the time he divorced Marva for the second time, Joe was a world class hero—and the ''sepia queen'' of Hollywood was the beautiful Lena Horne. For a short time their ''duet'' extended beyond party fun.

9

"Joe wants to get married," Roxborough said.

"It'll wait," Mike Jacobs countered. "Where is he?"

Joe was in Detroit. He had been enjoying himself at home with the family. Marva, too, was spending some time in Detroit, and Joe was seeing a lot of her. But it was time to get back to serious training—the Levinsky fight was past a knockout in round one, Joe throwing a maximum of ten punches. Now it was getting on to *Baer* hunting time, and Jacobs and Roxborough and Black and Chappie wanted him back at Pompton Lakes. Marriage would simply have to wait a bit longer.

After watching Baer against Braddock, Joe had little regard for the former as a boxer. Yet he trained earnestly, methodically for the fight, the one he'd been waiting for since even before Carnera.

"Ain't nobody gonna tell me these two are the two best fighters in the world," Joe had commented after the Baer-Braddock bout. The newspapers had picked it up, printed it. Baer read it and, while in training at Speculator, New York, reflected on the meaning of Louis' contempt for his ability as a fighter. Baer had never really taken boxing seriously. Now, faced with the prospect of going against Louis, the Brown Bomber's comment gnawing at him, Baer earnestly set himself to the task of achieving peak boxing form. When reporters visited him at his camp, Baer spoke boldly and with assurance of his impending victory.

At Pompton Lakes, Joe remained as laconic as usual. He was outwardly unconcerned. Inwardly, however, he was doubly anxious for September 24, 1935 to arrive, doubly because it was to be his wedding day also.

The weigh-in was scheduled for noon on the day of the fight. Baer was late—a strategic maneuver? When he finally swaggered into the weigh-in room, he tried to upset Louis. Joe had remained unconcerned throughout the time lapse, spent most of it reading a newspaper. When he ignored Baer, the other fighter became reflective, seemed to find new cause for alarm in the Brown Bomber's calmness.

That same evening, two hours before the flight, Joe slipped a four-carat diamond ring on Marva's fourth finger. The Reverend Trotter, Marva's brother, performed the ceremony. Immediately it was over, Joe stepped into a car and rode behind a siren-screaming police escort to Yankee Stadium.

Again Joe was sitting impatiently in the corner of a boxing ring, but less nervous this time, it seemed. It was almost as if he had a crystal ball this time, had seen the outcome of the fight and was only waiting for it to be over.

"Box him," Chappie advised. "Just stick and move, and hit him when he tries to throw his right. That'll stop him."

Joe listened, absorbed the words as the bell announcing round one sounded. It was just as Chappie had said: Baer represented only a minor threat to Louis. The Brown Bomber punished the man severely. In the fourth round, Baer went to the canvas under a two-handed attack and stayed there. Shaking his head from side to side, Baer took the count as an incredible shout sounded from the throats of the 88,150 fight fans in the ballpark.

In the fifteenth row, the new Mrs. Marva Louis finally relaxed. It had been a busy day. Not only had Joe married her and won the fight, but had earned $240,000 from the gross receipts of $1,000,832. The Brown Bomber had brought the million-dollar gate back to boxing.

In Harlem and other black ghettos all over America there was celebration. Blacks ran through the streets cheering their new brother-hero. Joe was indeed a symbol of a better way of life for black people, a far away dream. If it was possible for one black man, it was possible for all of them, the consensus seemed to say. There seemed to be a strange new hope born out of Louis' victory that somehow things would now get better for every black man.

There was more to come. The *trouble* was indeed brewing hot in Europe, Mussolini a la Carnera was merely a small part of what lay ahead on both the Atlantic and Pacific horizons. White hopes would come from everywhere—Schmeling foremost—and fall, and Louis would have to continue being the only black hope for millions of poverty stricken, ridiculed and oppessed Negroes. It was a hard championship to maintain.

Harder still for a simple farm boy from these cold and hard red clay hills of Alabama. Another puzzle was being formed piece by minute piece. It was all destined to come together on May 1, 1979. Like all great men, the world was being slowly eased upon Joe Louis' powerful shoulders.

Joe Louis was so popular by the early 1940s that children all over the world were named after him. And those that lived in parts of the Midwest could drink Joe Louis milk!

10

Another Christmas. . .years later. Louis had developed the habit of spending that particularly holiday with Martha and her aging mother in their Los Angeles apartment. It meant a great deal to Martha, and Joe often granted such concessions to make his wife happy.

However, just before the holiday, Joe phoned from New York. "I'm not coming home," he said. "You come to New York."

Martha had detected a strange tension in Joe's voice. "I've got an eighty-year-old mother," she shouted. "Besides, what the hell am I going to do sitting in a hotel room in New York on Christmas Eve?"

Joe insisted that there was no sense in flying all the

way to Los Angeles when he had to be back in New York the following week. It was a long trip both ways, one he could do without. There was simply no sense in it.

"Then you do what you please," Martha said. "I'm staying here with my mother."

When trying to decipher the events that ultimately led to Joe's illness, the commitment to the Colorado Psychiatric Hospital and later, Martha Louis often remembers that particular Christmas. Was it a sign of what was to come?"

"Maybe that was it," Martha would later admit. "Or maybe it could have been when Joe started to tell me he'd be arriving on one plane and I'd rush out to the airport and he wouldn't be on that plane at all. He'd go to another city instead. That happened a lot. It became a pattern of his operation. It started me to thinking."

Another meaningful development was the time Martha did go to New York to meet Joe, accompanied by Jacqueline, his daughter. As usual, they found Joe registered at the Park Sheraton where he normally rented a suite. An impromptu family reunion . . . until Joe left the hotel alone one evening and stayed out all night. Martha fretted and worried. In the morning, she began to search for her husband. She called friends. No one had seen Joe. She then visited some of his usual haunts but came away even more worried. When Joe did not return to their suite for the second night, Martha was too tense to sleep. She paced the floor. She considered calling the police but quickly rejected the notion because such might lead to bad publicity.

Suddenly, next morning, the door to their suite opened. Joe entered quietly. He looked a mess: sparse hair uncombed, clothes disheveled. "Where the hell have you been?" Martha shouted. "Joe, what happened to you?''

Joe tried to speak. He seemed confused. His words came in a faltering mumble, incoherent.

''Joe, you been in some sort of trouble?'' Martha was more frightened than angry now.

''I...I was in this place, and the police raided it,'' Joe managed at last.

''Didn't you tell them who you were?''

''They put all the others in one cell. They gave me a special cell,'' Joe answered.

''I don't believe you.'' Martha was furious again. ''You mean to tell me Joe Louis gets arrested and it doesn't get into the newspapers. Who you kidding?''

''That's what happened.''

What could be said? Either Joe's explanation was the product of delusion, irrationality, or he was lying. Martha could not for a minute believe what he said had happened actually happened, but she decided not to press the matter. There were *too many* strange things happening lately.

Suddenly Joe was composed. ''I'm sleepy,'' he said. ''Gonna try to sleep.''

Martha watched as he chose one of the two bedrooms facing the living room. Without removing his clothes, he dropped on the bed, and muttered, ''They better not start shooting the gas in here now.'' He got up, went to a table and took hold of two phone books. Then, picking up a pillow from the bed, he shoved the phone books into the pillowcase. Again he flopped on the bed. This time he place the weighted pillow over her head. ''That gas ain't gonna get me now,'' he mumbled. Then he slept.

Delusions? A persecution complex? Or was it the nightlife of New York City that kept Joe away from his wife and daughter for two days . . . perhaps Marion Eggberg. Or perhaps, following the two Schmeling fights and the international issues involved there, the causes that were fought and overcome in the ring, the stigma of the Nazi gas chambers actually had crept inside the powerful Brown Bomber's head. Joe was so many things to so many different people, and indirectly involved—mostly against his will—in so many damned causes.

Fighters come and fighters go, most falling beaten, some punchdrunk at the wayside, especially in Joe's heyday. Especially if the fighter happened to be a black man.

But Louis hung in there, in spite of a fight schedule that would have made the average boxer dizzy, and in spite of the odds against him becoming the first black heavyweight champion of the world since Jack Johnson. Jolting Joe, the farm boy from Alabama, made it to the top rung, slipped and climbed back up more times than any boxer than in recent history. Was it the strain of this that ultimately created incidents such as Martha Louis revealed? Was it the "I want, I need, and can I have" syndrome that overeager fans hefted on Joe—not maliciously, but overwhelmingly because Joe Louis was such an overwhelmingly champion.

Speculation all. In later years, Martha learned of Joe's sporadic romances. She was, as Joe realized the first time he saw her, a true lady. She turned away. Joe always came home to her and the children.

Whatever the true events behind the particular incident at the New York Sheraton, there was a strangeness building in Joe, mounting up. Martha was more aware of it because she was closest to him, and a man, even inadvertently, often reveals to the woman he loves things no one else is allowed to see.

11

Strange incidents seem to plague and sometimes pleasantly surprise the well-known . . . like meeting Lena Horne by chance through the owner of Harlem's Cotton Club, and Joe being offered his choice from the lineup she appeared in. There are unwritten benefits in a heavyweight champion's contract, and Joe, because of his simple, straightforward style, perhaps received more than most. Like the time just before the Max Baer fight when the Brown Bomber figured he had earned a big shiny new car, something extra fancy, and went out to buy one.

At the Buick showroom, the salesman who was up on the floor rushed to accommodate Joe. He had lauded the extra features of the black Buick limousine with white wall tires. The car had a mahogany bar built into the back seat. The bar fascinated Joe. Although the Bomber did not drink, that built-in bar had a look of class he couldn't resist.

While Joe was toying with the car, pulling dashboard knobs and flicking switches, the salesman excused himself and rushed to accommodate a very good-looking white woman with blonde hair. They talked. The salesman returned to where Joe was still fiddling with the car.

"I like this car," Joe said. "I want to buy it."

"The, ah...the lady has already purchased the car for you." The salesman grinned knowingly.

Joe's mind flashed immediately to photographs of Jack Johnson that had appeared in national newspapers. He heard Roxborough, Black, Blackburn and Jacobs warn about having his picture taken with white women—*Mr. Charlie* never liked that, no way! But there were no cameras anywhere to be seen, and what the hell can a man do when the lady insists and is charming as all get up. Joe took the car and promised the woman two ringside tickets for the Max Baer fight. Thereafter, he received a new Buick every Christmas for the next five years.

The way Joe sees the incident, "The lady was a very important white woman and I was a very important black man. She taught me the word for many of the things I'd been doing all along. The word was 'discretion.' And we were 'discreet' the several times we met during those five years."

While in training for the Baer fight at Pompton Lakes, Roxborough and Black hired a combination secretary-tutor for Joe. Russell Cowans was a short man, five-foot-five, and a college graduate. He was a sportswriter for the *Detroit Chronicle* and ideal for the job. Each day after roadwork, Cowans primed Joe in grammar and arithmetic.

The mail was pouring in. A lot of it was from black folks praising Joe, saying as how they felt so much better about themselves because of the way he was fighting and handling his personal life. There were letters from black kids wanting to know all about his training schedule, and saying as how they wanted to be just like him. It gave Joe a good feeling. And it was times like these that he regretted not having paid more attention in school; not being able to write back the way he wanted to. Occasionally even a white kid sent him a letter expressing the same sentiments as the black kids.

Cowans probed. He had sent a written breakdown of segments of Joe's life to newspapers all over the country. He made Joe remember things he had forgotten, made him see himself in relation to what he was doing, what he was accomplishing, and in relation to what such action could mean to other people—particularly black people. It wasn't easy. Joe had set out to be a fighter, nothing more. Now he was becoming a good will ambassador for millions of people he had never met. He was at once pleased and confused by the responsibility.

Joe Louis was now all over the sports pages, and often in front page headlines. Some newsmen were calling him a "born killer," stretching truths and telling lies that upset Joe. "Keep calm," Roxborough and Black told him. "Be glad you're important enough for people to talk and write about you. Means they'll be spending their money to come see the 'born killer' ".

What really upset Joe, however, was the news item that quoted Jack Johnson as saying he, Joe Louis, was "merely a flash in the pan." Johnson reputedly went on to state that at his age of fifty-seven, he would have done just as well against Joe as Carnera and Levinsky. Johnson supposedly went on to say that Joe's stance was all wrong, and pointed out other faults in his boxing style. But Johnson had always been a big mouth. It was one of the reasons the white promoters had been so dead set against booking another black heavyweight into Madison Square Garden. Joe didn't know what to believe: the papers or his respect for Jack Johnson. It was hard to believe that the man who had visited his camp, laughed and joked with him, would say such things to the press.

After the news release, in discussing it with Chappie, Louis learned that Jack Johnson may have had other motives in saying what he did to the press—if indeed he had said it. It had to do with Chappie, not Joe—an incident in 1908, before Joe was born. In those days, before Johnson was champion, he used to train in a gym in Philadelphia. One day he need a sparring partner. Chappie happened to be there and said he'd go a few founds even though he weighed only 135. Johnson, no doubt, saw Chappie as no threat at all. He was a little guy, a *wiry* little guy even then, and he bloodied Johnson's nose. Angry, Johnson tried to knock him out but couldn't do it. Johnson got madder and madder and more and more embarrassed.

Years later when Chappie was released from prison after serving his sentence for murder, the fight crowd people got together to give him a benefit to get him started again. The group asked Johnson to participate. He refused, called Chappie every variety of S.O.B. imaginable. Chappie thought that Johnson may have said the things he did to the press to inadvertently get back at him through Joe. They already knew that Johnson was a sneaky manipulator: he had gone to Roxborough while Joe was in training for the Carnera fight, told the manager that he wanted to be Joe's trainer and to throw Chappie out. Roxborough set him straight, told him how he had held up the progress of black people for years with his *nigger style* attitude and that he was no longer welcome in the Joe Louis camp. Johnson returned to his job as strong man in Robert Ripley's Flea circus, a good place for that type of nigger to be.

After that, Joe saw very little of Jack Johnson around camp or elsewhere.

The day after the Max Baer fight, Joe read in the papers that Baer had said he, Joe, was just lucky to have won, had no business in the same ring with him. He had also made several choice comments about the Negro race and Joe's personal life. Joe couldn't understand Baer's attitude, just as he had found it difficult to understand Jack Johnson's comments to the press. Joe was not like that: mean! At least not *outside* the ring.

But it was their honeymoon, his and Marva's. She had looked like something from a fairy tale book in her white silk gown, long train trimmed in ermine, and a bunch of little white flowers in her small hand. They had been married at 7:45. Joe had left for the match with Baer at 8:00. Two victories for Joe in one evening. The first, getting Marva. Second was the knockout over a popular ex-champion. He was feeling good, looking finer than ever before in his career.

Joe and Marva stayed in New York for the first two weeks of their marriage. It became a chore to show her the city Joe had learned to love. Fans followed them everywhere. If they went to the movies, they had to sneak out before the show was over or be swamped with well-wishers. Plus the girls. They still crowded Joe as if Marva was not there. They escaped to Hollywood finally on an invitation by Bill Robinson to watch him and Shirley Temple make a movie.

On October 31, 1935, Joe and Marva flew to St. Louis to watch John Henry Lewis win the light heavyweight title from Bob Olin in fifteen rounds. It was an important match: John Henry was a black man, Bob Olin was white. Moreover, Henry was managed by Gus Greenlee, a black Pittsburg numbers boss. Greenlee also owned the Pittsburg Crawfords baseball team in the Negro National League. On the night he won the championship, Henry became the only black man with a black manager to hold a boxing title. It was a breakthrough, and a break for Joe. Now he would not be the *only* one.

Now even Roxborough, Black and Chappie knew it was time to go after Braddock. There was not much in the way of heavyweights standing between Joe and the champion, and if the Bomber beat them all, or as many as necessary before a contract was urged. Braddock could not refuse the match.

Max Schmeling was beginning to loom on the European horizon: early on in 1935 after Joe had beaten Hans Birkie and Lee Ramage, Schmeling, the former heavyweight champion, made it known publicly that he was ready to shoot for the title he had held from 1930 to 1932. He and Braddock seemed to be Joe's only real opposition.

Also early on in 1935, in March, Steve Hamas fought Schmeling in Hamburg, Germany. Hamas had beaten Schmeling badly in 1934. In the rematch, however, Schmeling had worked his way into a challenger's position through the Hamas fight. He banked that position through beating the hell out of Paulino Uzcudun in Berlin in July, 1935. Schmeling had opened the door to come back to America.

Roxborough and Black made a smart move. They offered Uzcudun $19,000 to come from Spain to go against Joe at Madison Square Garden. Schmeling had knocked the man out in twelve. Roxborough and Black figured Joe could do the same work in maybe half the number of rounds. Uzcudun accepted, and the match was scheduled for December 13 at the Garden.

Now it was back to Pompton Lakes and more serious training. Joe had come a long way. There was still a ways to go, but now they could all see the pot of gold at the end of the fight ring rainbow.

Schmeling appeared one day at the camp, pensively watching Joe train. Joe noted that the German was about his same height, same weight. He grinned to himself. He and Schmeling exchanged steady glances. "I'll take him," Joe muttered. It was at the training session that Schmeling saw the flaw in Joe Louis' style, the mysterious "sumting" he mentioned to newsmen afterward. Joe and Cowan laughed when they read it in the newspapers.

There was nothing going to stand between Joe and the championship. He decided when he stepped through the ropes in the Garden on December 13. Especially not Uzcudun. He waited impatiently for the bell announcing the start of round one. When it clanged, Uzcudun came out of his corner in a crouch, stooped and lunged forward. His face was hidden behind his gloves and crossed arms. Chappie had told Joe to be careful not to break his hands on the man's head.

Joe jabbed lightly and carefully. He knew after the first round that Uzcudun would try to go distance, was boxing it that way . . . gloves and crossed arms. He was afraid of Joe, scared to stand toe-to-toe.

Joe continued to follow Chappie's instructions . . . jab . . . jab and wait for an opening. The openings always came, he knew by now. Sometimes in the second, sometimes in the third. This time it came in the fourth. Uzcudun's guard dropped for a moment and Joe hit him a hard right to the jaw. He countered with a left hook. Joe banged a right over the left, and Uzcudun was down.

The crowd roared . . . Brown Bomber, Brown *Bomber*! But Uzcudun was up after an eight-count. Joe stepped in, hit him with a left and a right to the jaw, sent him sprawling into the ropes. Uzcudun's face was split open and some of his gold teeth lay bloodied on the canvas. Referee Donovan counted him out on his feet in two minutes and thirty-two seconds of the fourth round. It was Joe's twenty-sixth straight victory as a professional.

After the fight, Whitey Bimstein, the trainer who worked in Uzcudun's corner that night, said he had never seen anyone hit anybody as hard as Joe laid it to the Spaniard in that bout. It had taken Joe only four rounds where Schmeling needed twelve. He and Schmeling were running neck and neck for a shot at Braddock's title.

Quickly Mike Jacobs began to negotiate for a Schmeling-Louis match. Roxborough and Black refused to stand still: they arranged for Joe to go against Charley Retzlaff in Chicago on January 17, 1936 . . . too late to honor the clause written into the Schmeling-Louis contract for June 19 at Yankee Stadium.

Schmeling's manager, Joe Jacobs, demanded the clause: neither boxer could fight for six months before the scheduled match at Yankee Stadium. They conceded that the Retzlaff fight had already been contracted before the signing date of the Schmeling bout, but there were to be no matches for Joe after that one. The clause meant little to Joe at that time. Later, after his defeat by Schmeling, he and Chappie and his managers realized that Joe Jacobs may have negotiated a fast one on them. Both Jacobs and Schmeling were sly enough to realize that Joe had fought two or three fights a month throughout his professional career. It was the best way to maintain timing and coordination. Six months away from the ring was the best way to blow it.

The break seemed just fine to Joe at the time. He went to New York to train for the Retzlaff fight. There he met Ed Sullivan, a young sportswriter for the *New York Daily News*. They quickly became friends, and Ed introduced Joe to golf. First the reporter brought Joe books on the game, then he brought clubs to the house. Joe was swinging, slicing, hooking and putting all over the apartment. Nineteen thirty-five had been one hell of a year for Joe—Marva and all those knockouts. Now, with almost six months out of the ring after the Retzlaff fight ahead, he began to develop the sport that would become his second passion.

*In 1942, Champion Joe Louis joined the United States Army.
He hoped, along with Brig. General Benjamin O. Davis, also
black, that his presense would help defeat both facism and
racism.*

12

On January 17, 1936, as if determined to make the new year his best year thus far in boxing, Joe knocked Retzlaff out in one minute and fifty-six seconds of the first round. It was his fastest knockout yet—two left hooks and a right uppercut, and *bang*! But before it ended, Retzlaff had hit Joe with a right to the chin that was the hardest punch he had taken in his professional career.

No matter. The months stretched lazily ahead to the Schmeling fight, and Joe was off to Hollywood for his debut as a movie star. Elliott Shanburg and Leo Golden were producing a film called *The Spirit of Youth*, and Joe—of all people, he thought—had been chosen to play the lead. The movie was about a young poor boy who started out as a dishwasher and worked his way up to champion of the world. Edna Mae Harris was Joe's leading lady, and the vacation away from the ring seemed, at the time, just the thing he and Marva needed. Like New York and Harlem, it taught Joe more about life . . . this time life in the motion picture profession, like the fact that Edna Mae Harris was a beautiful black woman.

Good-looking black women were lucky to get parts as maids in those days. If you were black, you also had to be big and fat, talk with a Southern accent, roll your eyes and act dumb. Then you usually got a part in a Tarzan movie—feathers and war paint and spears—and simply could not get along without some screaming at white men. It was hard on those black folks who wanted to be in the movies. Like Mantan Morley, and those other Negro actors who played the Charley Chan movies, and kept saying things like, "Feets don't fail me now" during the scarey parts. It was, Joe thought, a damn shame that black America was being portrayed as a group of shuffling males, and females who worked their pretty way up from chamber maid to fat house momma.

There were girls in Hollywood, too. Eager starlettes. Joe could never resist a pretty girl with a sexy sparkle in her eye. One such girl was Sonja Henie. She was about the cutest little white girl Joe had ever met—pug-nosed, blonde hair and bright blue eyes. From Norway, she had won the Women's Figure Skating Gold Medal in three straight Olympics. Joe remembered what Roxborough and Black and Chappie had warned about black men and white women. He and Sonja managed to keep their affair secret from the prying eyes of Hollywood.

Marva? Marva was beautiful and Joe loved her. She was his chosen wife. But there were so many pretty girls itching for a taste of the upcoming champion. Whenever Joe felt guilty about the affairs, he simply went out to buy Marva an expensive gift to make up for it.

And then Schmeling!

May 13 was Joe's twenty-second birthday. There was a party. Nat Fleischer, editor of *Ring Magazine*, gave Joe a gold decorated belt: Joe Louis had been picked by the magazine as the Number One Boxer of 1935.

Jimmy Braddock was one of the notables at the party. After the belt was presented, Braddock came up to Joe to wish him a happy birthday. Then he said, "Joe, you must be running from me. Why don't you come after me? I mean, I'm the champion and all and here I am coming to you."

"Soon as I finish Schmeling, look out," Joe replied. "Look out because you looking at the next heavyweight titleholder."

The party continued, Joe on top of the world. He was Mr. Big at twenty-two. Important people were his friends . . . Johnny Dundee, Tony Canzoneri, Tommy Loughran and others were present at the party. He was feeling real good, looking exceptionally fine. Schmeling? Shoot! Joe knew he could win any match he wanted to, had proven it time and again. First Schmeling, then Braddock, and then . . . ? They could never find anyone to beat him. He was certain of that. At least no time soon.

But it was to training camp soon after the party. Joe was certain it was going to be a lot of hard work for nothing; he thought sure he could name the round in which Schmeling would fall. He was so certain of impending victory that he cut his training sessions short to play golf, and instead of gradually working up to his physical peak, he began to lose weight. It was easy enough to lose, but impossible to put back on before the fight, he learned. He was weakened, and he was about to step into the ring for what was his most important fight to date.

Chappie told him. Chappie told him lots of things . . . like *stay away from girls!* But there were so many of them after the upcoming champion. So many that Chappie actually had to take a stick and threaten them away at one time. This was training camp, and somehow Joe seemed to have forgotten what that meant. Somehow his ego had gotten in the way of the path to the heavyweight championship.

Twice Roxborough had to chase Joe off the golf course: he was dehydrating under the hot sun. The four pounds he ran off each morning through running was not being gained back through the food and rest afterward, and the whole camp—all except Joe—was beginning to worry. Joe had lost eighteen pounds in five weeks, too fast a reduction for anyone not on a crash diet and perhaps fatal for a heavyweight fighter.

Chappie kept warning Joe about Schmeling's righthand punch. Joe ignored him: he had handled righthand punchers before, no problem. He was twenty-two, after all, not some little kid who didn't know what he was doing. He was full of spunk even after Bill Farnsworth, one of the Hearst sportswriters, came to the camp to watch him train, and said afterward, "I'm betting on Schmeling."

On the Sunday before the fight, one of Joe's sparring partners, Salvatore Ruggerillo, a boxer with a righthand punch like Schmeling's, quit after the first round. Joe was still raring to go. He dusted through the others quickly, still full of steam. He was hell on wheels that day, felt he could have kept going all afternoon and beat anyone. The problem was that his training was off, and he reached his peak five days before the fight.

The day of the weigh-in finally arrived. The Hippodrome still stank of the animal odor left from the circus show called *Jumbo,* starring Jimmy Durante. Schmeling hadn't arrived in from Napanoch, New York. It was raining to beat all hell up there, and he was coming by car. Nervous? Joe? He went to Durante's old dressing room to take a nap.

Finally, Schmeling arrived. The weigh-in took place: Schmeling at 192, Louis at 196. Then the fight was postponed for a day because of rain.

Again one wonders what Joe would have done had he had a crystal ball through which to see into the future. Would he have trained harder, given up the golf to concentrate on his trade? Or perhaps youth would have won out even then. Perhaps even champions have to learn lessons the hard way.

Mike Jacobs had expected a crowd of 85,000, but there were only 50,000 tickets sold as of five days before the fight. A Jewish organization had sent out flyers to local storekeepers, it seemed. The message was to boycott the fight because Schmeling represented Nazi Germany. The news made Joe uneasy. It was the only thing that bothered him, his only uncertainty, not even that could dampen his certainty of victory.

The weather was still bad on the day of the fight . . . cloudy and looked like more rain. When the sky finally did turn blue, there were flashes of lightning. Everything about the match seemed ill-fated, including the fact that only 40,000 people showed up to watch out of the 50,000 tickets sold. Even the fact that Schmeling was a ten-to-one underdog seemed a reverse ominous omen to all but Joe.

Schmeling entered the ring first. Instructions were given by the referee. Chappie whispered the same instructions he had been shouting at Joe throughout the training camp . . . *watch out for his right, don't drop your guard*. Then the bell announcing round one rang and Joe was on his own.

The rest is history . . . Louis down in the fourth for the first time in his professional career. In the sixth, Freddie Guinyard escorted Joe's mother from the stadium while she prayed, "My God, my God, don't let him kill my child." In the twelfth, Louis was down for the count, Schmeling victorious. It was a sad day in Harlem, in Detroit, in Chicago. Wherever black people grouped together it was like a monument torn down by a man who supposedly represented the philosophy of white supremacy.

When Joe finally came round and stared at himself in the mirror, he could not believe the image that stared back. He could not see his lashes; his forehead was swollen down to his eyelids, a big lump on his left cheek. His lips were swollen, too . . . like the big red lips on one of those silly nigger dolls they made in the image of black fighters. Now, he remembered all the things he should have done, all Chappie's warnings. But there was no going back to do it over again, no way. Now he would have to inch his way up the ladder again, prove himself worthy. It was not the last Max Schmeling had heard from Joe Louis.

13

Later, Many years later. Joe was in Las Vegas with Martha, his third wife, in a suite at a Caesar's Palace. Joe seemed deeply distressed...not merely over the business, but a deeper, secret agitation. Martha's intuition told her she would have to find out for herself what was bothering him. Her suspicious were further aroused by a phone call, after which Joe appeared even more agitated.

"What's the matter, Joe?" Martha tried. "You get some girl pregnant?"

"Wish I was as good a man as you give me credit for," Joe replied quickly.

"Oh, come, come," Martha said. "Why don't you just tell me the truth?"

Joe forced a tight smile. "Ain't nothing to it."

Fuming, Martha contained her anger, composed herself. Intuition told her to search further, but secretly. Quietly she listened while he told her about the sports dinner he had to fly to New York to attend. "Why don't you call the Park Sheraton and get me a reservation?" he suggested.

Martha complied, asked the hotel desk to reserve the room on the 24th floor that they had previously occupied. She had planned to join Joe almost immediately, but then something came up in Los Angeles that demanded attention. Joe left alone. Martha gave him enough time to arrive, settle in, then called him. She was told by the desk that he was not registered in the room on the 24th floor, but rather, in room 1026.

New suspicions were now aroused. Why had Joe done that? Then, instead of flying back to Vegas from New York, Joe went to Oakland to attend "another important sports function." Martha happened to be in the vicinity and greeted him at the airport.

"Hello, Joe," she called when she spotted Louis. "Have a good trip?"

Surprised, Joe replied, "It was all right."

"You had a different room, didn't you?"

"Yeah, they knew I liked this other room," Joe said.

Martha let it drop for the moment. Some time later, however, both she and Joe took a trip to Miami and stayed at the Hilton. Just before Valentine's day, several cards arrived for Joe. The cards were addressed *For Daddy*, and the envelopes bore the number of the room in which they were staying. One was signed by someone named Marie.

"What about these?" Martha asked.

"Don't know anything about them," Louis insisted.

"Now look," Martha tried. "You're talking to me.

It's impossible for someone to know your room number when you got here yesterday unless . . . !''

"You explain it," Louis said.

"Well, let me tell you something. You would have had to be in contact with the person who knew the room number. That's all I got to say," Martha fumed.

Again the matter was dropped for the moment. Then they left for New York, registered at the Park Sheraton. Once back in New York, Martha managed to get the story from one of Joe's cronies who had gotten it from Joe during one of his more talkative moments. Again she confronted Joe: "Joe, look, you're talking to me. For once, tell me the truth. Not only am I your wife, I'm your friend. What about this baby that was born on December 2, 1967?"

"I ain't seen that girl but once," Louis said coldly. "She's a $50 trick. And I've never seen the baby."

"Great!" Martha said.

The matter was dropped again for a few days. "Look, Joe, let me make deal with you," Martha offered at last. "Since you don't know where the baby is and you've seen this woman but once, what about me talking to her?"

"Yeah, you can talk to her. Sure," Joe replied. He was not aware that Martha already knew that the women was living in the same hotel, in Room 1026 . . . the same room Joe had occupied when he had been to New York alone a short time before.

Silence fell over them. It was Sunday, March 3, 1968. They had nothing planned, were merely sitting around the suite resting. Suddenly Joe said, "Martha, I think I'll go on up to the Red Rooster in Harlem."

"Good, I'll go with you," Martha suggested.

"Don't you think I'm big enough to go by myself?"

Martha admitted that he was old enough. Then she

added, "You'll probably be gone by the time I get back. I'm going right downstairs now to have breakfast."

"I'll wait until you get back," Joe hastily amended. "No hurry."

Martha got the picture full and clear. Joe had absolutely no intention of visiting the Red Rooster in Harlem. What he was planning was to take the elevator down to the tenth floor and visit Room 1026. But he did not want to chance running into Martha while she was out of the suite because there was always a chance, however slim, that he would be spotted and caught in another lie.

When Martha returned from breakfast, Joe said, "Okay, I'm going. Be home about three."

At four o'clock Joe still had not returned. Martha was fuming. "That man must think I'm the biggest fool in this world," she muttered to herself. "He's got a girl in this hotel and he's telling me he's going up to Harlem." She picked up the phone and called Room 1026. A woman answered. "Listen, I want to tell you one thing," Martha said tightly. "I know Joe's down there, and I have made up my mind exactly what I'm going to do. You just tell that to Joe."

Martha then placed a call to a friend and ex-sparring partner of Joe's, told him that she knew all about the baby, and that he could tell Joe so for her. She knew the man would call Joe immediately. Then one of two things would happen, she felt certain. Either Joe would come upstairs to face her sheepishly or rush away somewhere. She hoped for the former. But no sooner had the friend talked to Louis on the phone and hung up, Joe was off to the airport and Detroit. Martha spent a sleepless night waiting for him to return.

Another side of Joe Louis. Like a many-faceted diamond in the rough, the champion had many faces—some good, some not so pleasant to look at. So many people knew him as so many things. It had become part of is makeup: all things to all people. Being heavyweight champion of the world is no simple task for a boy whose first waking desire was to farm his own land in the red clay hills of Alabama.

The day following Joe's flight to Detroit, March 4, 1968, was an historic one in boxing. The new Madison Square Garden was to open, and Louis had been invited to be introduced from the ring before the main event between Joe Frazier and Buster Mathis. Joe never showed up. Neither did Martha. She was in her suite at the Park Sheraton, talking to the girl in Room 1026 on the phone. "You come up here or I'll come down to you," she was saying. "Don't make no difference to me."

"I'll come up there," the girl agreed at last.

Soon there was a knock at the door. Martha answered it. "I'm Marie Johnson," the girl standing in the outer hall said. She motioned to the young man who had accompanied her. "I brought him along. I was afraid something could happen. I told him I owed you a hundred dollars and I don't have it. He can be here while we talk."

Martha stepped aside, invited her in. She eyed the other woman. Marie Johnson was small, thin. She had a behind no bigger than a man's hand. "I'm going to talk frankly to you, Marie," Martha said. "It was no accident on your part. What you did, going and having a baby, was no accident. And you don't even know if it's Joe's baby."

"Them things happen," Marie said.

"I'm not going to argue," Martha quickly added. "What I'm concerned about is the baby."

"He's all right," Marie assured. "Got good care for him with my family."

"I'd like to take him," Martha Monroe Jefferson Louis said. "We can give him a lot of love and protection." She knew the girl must have been in prostituion and maybe prison. She felt Joe's baby deserved something better than that.

"One thing, don't get on Joe when you see him," Marie said. "He was awful jittery yesterday when he found out you know about the baby. Just forget about everything."

"He's my husband. I'll handle him."

"He told me a lot of nice things about you," Marie offered. "About how his children like you very much and you go to church. But the only thing is you don't have enough time for him."

Martha smiled: her poor, neglected Joe. She and Marie talked for more than an hour. Marie was twenty-three. Born in Steubenville, Ohio, she had moved with her family to the metropolitan area and had been on her own since she was thirteen. At the time she met Joe, she was on parole from the women's prison at Bedford Hills, New York. Joe had been introduced to her in a Manhattan cocktail bar where she once worked as a waitress.

When they had finished talking, it was agreed that Martha would take the baby. They parted friends.

Soon after Marie left the suite, the phone rang. It was Joe from Detroit.

"When you coming back here?" Martha wanted to know.

"I'll be there tomorrow," Joe promised. It was almost as if nothing unusual had happened. That was the way Joe was.

Bits and pieces of the jigsaw puzle. 1934 to 1970, 1935 to 1968. All of it Louis. All of it part of one of the greatest heavyweight champions the world has ever known. There were no crystal balls for Joe to peek into, and no road map to follow up to the top. All of it he did himself and accomplished the hard way. In the ring, there was no doubt of his ability. Outside the ropes, he was as human as the rest of us.

Martha? As Joe had realized when they met, the woman had class. She had studied law throughout her early years, was a member of the California bar and still acted as defense counsel in many criminal cases. It was her training in law that had enabled her to put the pieces of her own jigsaw puzzle together, and come up with Marie Johnson and the baby. What could be more fitting than the Brown Bomber being out-pointed by his own wife.

March 27, 1945: Judge John Sbarbaro granted Marva Trotter Louis an uncontested divorce on charges of desertion. They remarried the next year, divorced a second time in 1949.

14

Nineteen thirty-nine. Joe was in training for the John Henry Lewis fight when Marva called from home. God, she'd had a miscarriage even before she had known she was pregnant, and needed him. Thing is, Joe could not go home, could not break training. He had done that once . . . before the first Schmeling fight, and he never again wanted to see the face that had looked back at him from the dressing room mirror. Henry was no bum.

On January 25, 1939, the weigh-in took place. It was to be the first major fight between two blacks since the days of slavery, and the newspapers were all over Louis and Henry. Joe had heard that Henry couldn't see laterally out of one eye and was worried about what to do with the information. He and John Henry were friends, but he couldn't go easy on the other fighter because of that.

Joe weighed in at 200¼ pounds, Henry at 180¾. Everything seemed to be in Joe's favor in this one.

Joe stepped into the ring that night with the thought that he would not punish John Henry, rather get it over with as quickly possible. The bell rang. Joe shuffled forward with grim determination written all over his face. Bang . . . Henry was done. Then twice more. In two minutes and twenty-nine seconds of the first round, referee Arthur Donovan stopped the first because Henry simply could not get up again. Joe was unhappy about having to beat his friend so badly. But he knew John was on his way out of the fight game, and at least he'd had the glory of a match against the Heavyweight Champion.

Back in Chicago, Joe was greeted by a letter from the doctors at the Mayo Clinic where Marva had gone after the miscarriage. The gist of the letter was that Marva should not have children: she was unnerved by the way they lived, needed more "stability" and more companionsip from her husband. If not, she might eventually suffer a nervous breakdown. The doctors had written letters to Roxborough and Black as well, and the three of them and Chappie sat down to hash it out.

Roxborough and Black came up with a plan to buy the Spring Hill Ranch outside Detroit. They figured it would be a great place to train, Joe would be closer to home and Marva, and the place would at least pay for itself. Joe talked to Marva about it and she seemed happy. Joe was trying. He was a big man with big appetites, but he didn't want to hurt Marva any more than she had already been hurt through the miscarriage. He told her she could build a fancy house on the ranch grounds, and perhaps they would live there when he retired. The idea sounded good even to Joe. And the ranch . . . there must have been at least 100 dogs there, and there was a big herd of Hereford cows. A man with some money, a beautiful wife and a couple of cute kids could lead a good clean lifestyle there. Joe bought the place for $100,000.

Marva, it turned out, was anemic as well as unnerved. The doctors prescribed a few ounces of Virginia Dare wine along with her other medication. Joe, not wanting his wife to become an alcoholic, took to measuring out the dosage three times a day. In later years, they would laugh about the incident, because it was Joe, not Marva, who had to worry.

The fight business went on in spite of miscarriages and prescribed home-life and companionship. Joe was to meet Jack Roper on April 17 in Los Angeles. He had not fought a match there since he knocked out Lee Ramage in 1935.

Roper had a powerful lefthand hook. It was what Joe was watching for when he stepped through the ropes for the match. The fight was over fast: knockout by Louis in the first round. But damned if Roper didn't nearly knock Joe down with a left hook before the Bomber got to him. A southpaw, it took Joe a minute or two to catch on to the reverse movements and get through the man's guard, and then *zappo!*

After the fight, both Louis and Roper on the air, the announcer asked Roper what had happened . . . Howard Cosell style. Roper said, "I zigged when I should have zagged." Joe always remembered him as a funny man.

Then came "Two-Ton" Tony Galento of Orange, New Jersey. Tony was five-foot-nine, 225 pounds and looked like a beer barrel. He was the furthest thing from being "in shape" that a boer can become . . . roly-poly

Tony. He was a saloon keeper, and it looked like he had a drink with every customer who came into the place. Tony said all kinds of nasty things about Joe before the fight, even called the Bomber on the telephone to insult him. Tony swore he had the fight in the bag, had Joe's number. It annoyed Joe at first. "But then I got to like the son of a bitch," the Bomber admitted in later years. "He had style and what they're calling 'charisma' nowadays."

The fight was scheduled for June 28, 1939, at Yankee Stadium. It was a fair sized crowd—35 to 40,000 people. People like a clown, something different. Tony fit both categories. Joe knew the man was a street brawler, and could be dangerous. His ring record proved that, and he staggered Joe with a hard left in the first round. Then he hit Joe with a right and a left to the jaw, and everything glazed over.

"He's strong, but a bluff," Chappie said between rounds. "Box him."

In the second round, Joe hit him so hard that Galento was almost lifted off the floor. He went down—no class, a bluff. He came up off the canvas before the eight-count that any educated fighter would have taken.

In the third round, Galento came out of his corner bleeding from the eye, nose and mouth. Joe figured he had him, got too confident—a bad fault that kep cropping up throughout his career. Galento hit him with a left hook that sent him to the canvas.

Really angry now, Joe went after the man like a programmed fighting machine. Galento was reeling and rocking. Joe kept at him . . . jab . . . jab, flurry. Finally, after another heavy barrage by Louis, "Two-Ton" Tony fell back and down. The whole ring shook as he hit the canvas. Referee Arthur Donovan pulled Joe back and counted Galento out. The roar of the crowd somehow seemed subdued this time. Galento had a special appeal to a lot of white people. But Black was sure beautiful that night.

There was a break in the fight schedule giving time to be with Marva as the doctors had ordered. They spent a lot of time together at Spring Hill. The first United States Negro Horse Show was being held in July at the Utica Riding Club outside Detroit, and Joe was in it. Riding a horse named MacDonald's Choice, he took third place and won a yellow ribbon and $1,500. It seemed that Joe could not lose at anything these days.

Marva took to life at Spring Hill. She liked riding. When Joe bought two horses of their own, along with an English saddle from none other than Bing Crosby, it was decided that Marva would go to riding school once he returned to training. Eventually, Marva learned to ride well, both straight and sidesaddle. Joe picked up a new word: "equestrian." It seemed to suit Marva who looked great in riding clothes. It was a happy time. Marva seemed refreshed, and Joe was glad. There had been too few happy times together between bouts since their marriage.

A rematch with Bob Pastor had been scheduled for September 20, and it was back to training camp for Joe. He remembered that Pastor had made him look somewhat bad by running all over the ring and staying for ten rounds. This time, he determined, it was going to be different.

The fight was slated for Briggs Stadium in Detroit. It was Joe's first bout since he became Champion, and to make it an extra special attraction and draw a big gate, the match was scheduled to go twenty rounds. Another first: no heavyweight title bout had gone that many rounds since Jess Willard beat Jack Johnson in Cuba years before.

The Louis team learned that Pastor's trainer, Freddie Brown, had instructed his fighter to run int he first match. Brown knew there was no way his boy could last in slugging it out with Joe, no way. But Pastor was just as upset as Joe was with the bad showing he'd made in the first match. He was a slugger. This time, he vowed, he was not going to run and look scared.

"Don't chase that white boy all over the place this time," Chappie said on the night of the fight.

Joe didn't have to. When the bell rang for round one, Pastor came straight at him. Joe knocked him down . . . five times in the first two rounds. He was game, a different fighter this time, determined to make a good showing. He got in some good punches before Joe knocked him out in the fifth, settlin the stigma of their first match once and for all.

Then it was back to Spring Lake, Marva and more horse shows. And more ribbons for Joe's trophy room.

Nineteen-forty came with time to spare before Joe went into training for his fight with Arturo Godoy. Things were great between Joe and Marva, really fine. Then Lena Horne was back in town, in Detroit, singing her sweet songs with the Charlie Barnett band. She and Joe ran into each other at a friend's place, and Lena was more beautiful than ever. Soon they were planning all kinds of places and ways to meet. It was getting serious until Joe had to get back to New York and train for the Godoy fight.

From Argentina, Godoy turned out to be trouble. Joe had expected an easy match. Instead, the man stayed in a low crouch throughout the fight and went the fifteen rounds to a decision. Joe won, but barely, and looked worse than he had looked against Pastor in the first match. "It was like trying to fight someone on the floor," Louis commented after the fight and the close decision.

Roxborough and Black immediately moved for a rematch. It was scheduled for June 20, again in New York.

The city was like a magnet drawing Joe . . . Harlem . . . beautiful women. He could never get his fill of the latter, and a friend, a black man named Dickie Wells, a bona-fide playboy, made it even easier. It was Wells who introduced him to Lana Turner, and Wells who knew all the safe after-hours clubs around Manhattan. Joe was like an alcoholic coming off the wagon.

At the Cotton Club, Joe met Ruby Dallas, a dancer. He fell in love with her—big man, big appetite. It was like steak, lamb chops, chicken, apples and bananas. Joe needed each at a different time, but wanted them all. And it was easy for the Heavyweight Champion of Harlem as well as the world.

June 20 at Yankee Stadium, Joe was prepared for the rematch with Godoy. His sparring partners throughout training had been guys who fought in a crouch, hunch-backed closed to the canvas. Chappie had showed Joe how to straighten them up with uppercuts. When the bell rang for round one of the rematch, Godoy walked out to center ring and immediately went down into his awkward crouch. Joe went after him with lefts . . . banging . . . banging. Soon he had the man bleeding, hurt. Godoy went down finally in the sixth but was saved by the bell. He was down again in the eighth, up again after an eight-count and messy. He'd had it, Joe knew. *Bang!* Godoy down for the second time in the eighth and the fight was stopped by the referee. No question this time about Joe's ability to handle a fighter with a peculiar and hard-to-get-to style.

Another member of Joe's family was experiencing a victory about the same time. Baby-sister, Vunice, was graduating from Howard University. The ceremonies at Washington, D.C. were, Joe later admitted, the "most meaningful thing in his life." Joe had financed Vunice's schooling, and now, so proud he thought he might burst, the sister he had watched grow from a baby was saying she wanted to go on for her Master's degree. Joe presented her with a new Buick as a graduation gift, and said, "Go, baby sister, go. It's all on me."

Then it was back to Spring Hill for another horse show, Marva in the competition this time. Another win: Marva took the trophy in the jumping competition, and on a horse that nobody except Joe and the animal's trainer had been able to handle previously. Everywhere Joe looked, he had reason to be proud.

War was plaguing the world. Roosevelt was running for his third term in office against Wendell Willkie. Charles Roxborough, Roxy's brother, the first black senator from Michigan, was campaigning for Willkie and got Joe involved. Joe knew only that Willkie was running on the international wing of the Republican Party ticket out of Indiana and was thoroughly involved in civil rights. The Depression was easing up and black people were starting to get decent jobs as America prepared for the possibility of entering the war. Willkie promised more and better jobs for minorities, equal rights. That sounded fine to Joe. He began to appear along with Charles Roxborough at political rallies for Willkie.

Joe knew that Roosevelt was a fan of his, and that, as President, he had set up Welfare Relief programs that had helped many blacks make it through the Depression. But he had also promised things that never materialized. Now, Willkie was saying things like, "Every American is going to have a place in this country." Joe was recalling the trouble he'd had as a black man bucking the white fight promoters, and the really hard times that had put his daddy in a mental hospital because he'd bene unable to cope. There were lots of black folks who needed help and Willkie seemed to be the man who was going to give it to them.

When Roosevelt was elected to his third term in office, Joe felt the defeat as deeply as Wendell Willkie. But life went on: he, Joe, was still a champion, and he knew now that his personal campaign in the ring had given black people renewed pride in themselves. No matter his own hearty appetites, the public image he maintained was one of wholesomeness—not flaunting and boastful as Jack Johnson had been—and his sportsmanship and ring ethics were unimpeachable.

Joe had made a vow to himself, his trainer and managers, that he would be a "fighting" champion . . . not like some who had run all over the country to avoid fighting him. But there was nobody of notoriety left to go against in the heavyweight division. Mike Jacobs did, however, line up six matches, one a month beginning in January of 1941, and ending in June. One sportswriter called this parade the "Bum of the Month Club."

Well . . . ! Alexander the Great had started to cry when he had no more worlds to conquer, but not Joe. Although the competition was lacking, the fighters involved in what the press called the Bum of the Month Club were professionals all, and each was doing his best to make a living in the only way he knew how. Joe knew the dreams they had that kept them going: he'd had the same dreams himself as an upcoming heavyweight. Some would make a name for themselves, most would not, but they were honest fighters doing the best they could. There could only be one Joe Louis. Going against the Champion was, win, lose or draw, a distinction in and of itself. The sportswriter who had made the snide comment didn't seem to realize that any one of these fighters could get killed or maimed for life in the ring. It was not the easiest way in the world to put food on the table, not unless you happened to take the big prize.

The first in the "Bum of the Month Club" series was a fighter named Red Burman. The match was again held in New York City, and it was a knockout for Joe in the fifth round. As a fighter, Burman was as good as many of the other opponents Joe had faced in the ring. Problem was, nobody was as good as Joe.

Next came Gus Dorazio in Philadelphia on February 17. He was the best around Philly at the time. Joe knocked him out in the second round.

Then came Abe Simon on March 21 in Detroit, a scheduled twenty-rounder. Simon reminded Joe of Primo Carnera in his size and style. He managed to stick and stay until Joe knocked him out in round thirteen.

April 8 brought Tony Musto at St. Louis, Missouri. It was Joe's first appearance in St. Louis. Tony was a local boy who had been doing good around town. But his style was too predictable, and Joe seemed to toy with the man until he decided to knock him out in the ninth round.

Buddy Baer, the oldest brother of Max Baer, was next on the agenda. But between fights, Marva served Joe with divorce papers. There were just too many bad scenes between them—a Negro organization wanting to give Joe a plaque while he was in Philadelphia for the Dorazio fight, and he, Joe, in the company of another girl when he appeared to accept. Marva, coming up on stage to stand between the two, had hissed, "Bitch, move" to the other woman. Plus incidents before that at Spring Hill. It seemed Joe was always on the road or fooling around with some chippie, and Marva felt she deserved better. Marva wanted a *husband*.

Pride hurt, realizing that he had, in fact, put Marva through the hoops, Joe pleaded his case to her. He swore he would leave the ring soon and it would be just the two of them. Then he arranged for her to go on a Caribbean cruise with Roxborough's and Black's wives while he went back into training for Buddy Baer.

Baer was no easy opponent, notwithstanding the "Bum of the Month Club" stigma. He obviously remembered what Joe had done to his brother in 1935 and fought like hell. A brutal left hook sent Joe crashing through the ropes in the first round of the match in April. Joe took a four-count. Baer obviously thought he had the Bomber at that point, came on even stronger. He was as stubborn as Joe, slugging it out. Almost as if each punch he landed was for his brother—take *that!* He put a mouse under Joe's right eye in the third round, opened a cut under the Champion's left eye in the fifth.

The sixth round was a melee, Joe and Baer standing toe-to-toe. Finally, Joe knocked him down. Baer came staggering up at the count of seven, could not keep his footing and fell again. The crowd stood and roared as one voice. Baer stirred again at the count of nine. The bell ending the round sounded. Baer was up. There was so much noise that neither Joe nor Baer seemed to hear the bell or the referee's count, and Joe rushed in and dropped him with another devastating right. Baer's manager screamed for a disqualification. He had heard the bell.

When the bell announcing round seven rang, Baer's manager was in the ring demanding that Joe be disqualified for hitting after the bell. Baer himself was out on his feet, stumbling around in a daze. Referee Donovan ordered the fighter's manager out of the ring. He refused to move, and Donovan—the two men screaming in each other's face—disqualified Baer and his manager, instead of Joe. It was kind of an easy way out for Baer. Joe may have hurt him permanently had he answered the bell for the seventh round.

Marva had returned from her cruise and told Joe of the victory she had won. It seems that Bermuda was, at the time, a segregated place, and Marva and Roxborough and Black's wives had been mistaken for "suntanned" white women or something—something other than Negro. But one white man recognized Marva from newspaper photos, told her so and then told the management of the hotel where the girls were staying. Soon after, Marva got a call from the management saying as how they wanted her and her friends to vacate the rooms they had taken. "No way," Marva said. The only way she was leaving that room was if the police came and dragged her out physically. She and Joe laughed about it: there was no way the management wanted the scandal of having had the Heavyweight Champion's wife dragged from their respectable hotel. Marva had managed to integrate Bermuda.

Joe's next fight was against a tough, arrogant Irishman named Billy Conn, and it was back into training for the Bomber. The divorce was still up in the air. Conn had the talent needed to be heavyweight Champion of New York from 1939 to 1940. He had recently vacated that title to move up into the heavyweight division, spurred on, no doubt, by the memory of other great Irish champions from John L. Sullivan to Jimmy Braddock. He was competent. The "Bum of the Month Club" distinction simply did not fit.

146

What bothered Joe was the fact that Conn would be coming into the ring at 175 pounds. He was "press conscious," particularly after what the sportswriters had said about the string of six oponents. He did not want to read about "Louis, weighing in at over 200 pounds, beat Billy Conn..." after the fight, and so instead of his usual rest on the day before the match, Joe trained like all hell to come in at under 200.

At the weight-in: Conn 174, Louis 199½ pounds. But Joe felt depleated, no pep. Chappie had gotten angry over the foolish maneuver, told Joe so. But it was too late to reverse the thing now with the match scheduled for that night. Pride had pushed Joe into making what might be a fatal mistake.

June 18. There were 55,000 people present at the Polo Grounds when the fighters stepped into the ring. The bell rang. Joe went after the man who fought like an irritating mosquito—sting and run. Conn was fast. The weight difference worked well for him: Joe simply could not pin him down long enough to make the kill, and when he did land punches, the Irishman shook them off and danced away. By the fifth round, Joe had cut him over the right eye and over the nose. Conn's speed kept him out of reach of the knockout punch, and Joe was starting to have visions of his title being taken away.

By round eight, Joe seemed sluggish. He was tiring. The foolish maneuver on the last day of training was taking its toll—just as Chappie had warned—and Conn was growing more aggressive, faster, it seemed. He was smart: he refused to stand toe-to-toe with Joe, obviously knew what would happen if they slugged it out and was trying to go the distance.

At his corner at the end of the twelfth round, Chappie told Joe, "You're losing on points. You got to knock him out."

Joe gritted his teeth, determination sending strength through his body. The bell rang for round thirteen. Conn came out cocky. He was making the mistake so many other fighters had made against Joe before . . . overconfidence. They clinched at the center of the ring. Conn said, "Joseph, you're in for a tough fight tonight."

Joe punched the arrogant Irishman off, said, "We'll see." And then Conn did what he had been waiting for him to do—threw the long left hook. Joe countered immediately with a hard right to the head. Conn seemed to go numb. Almost as if someone had turned him off by remote control. Joe flurried . . . rights and lefts . . . rights and lefts. Billy Conn went down. Joe, the referee, Chappie and the spectator crowd watched the fighter try to get up. He simply could not make it. He was counted out in two minutes and fifty-eight seconds of the thirteenth round. It was Joe's eighteenth successful defense of his heavyweight title.

Ironic that Conn had been included in the "Bum of the Month Club." It was almost as if the pressmen who had started the shame wanted Joe to relax, and *zappo!* Conn had fought like the new *white hope.* Joe had learned again not to believe everything he read in the papers.

Reflecting after the fight, Joe realized that Conn might have taken the Heavyweight Crown from him if the man had continued to dance. The crowd at the Polo Grounds had cheered the white boy on as if they were compatible with the idea. It had been the other way around when Joe was the underdog. Now the fans seemed to want somebody new up there.

"Champions come and champions go," someone had once said about the fight game, "but the crowds are always there screaming for new blood."

15

Disturbed by his showing in the Conn fight, Joe wanted to get back into the ring again as soon as possible. A match was arranged with Jim Robinson for July 11. It was an exhibition bout held in Minneapolis: knockout for Joe Louis in the first round.

Lou Nova was next on the ring agenda. Lou was always talking about Yoga and his own "cosmic punch," and Joe had seen him fight Max Baer at Yankee Stadium in April, 1941. It had been Nova by a knockout in the eighth round. It was going to be a tough match, Joe knew. The papers kept talking about Nova's cosmic punch, and what it was going to do to Joe. Joe kept asking what in hell a cosmic punch was.

There were 56,000 people at the Polo Grounds in New

York on September 29 when the two stepped through the ropes. Nova answered the bell for round one in excellent form. He managed to give Joe a rough time throughout the early rounds, but in round six, the Bomber caught him square on the chin with a solid right hand. Nova went down for a nine-count, wobbled onto his feet. He was game. But Referee Donovan stopped the fight a few seconds before the end of the round, and so much for cosmic punches where Jolting Joe Louis was concerned.

Newsmen and fans kept asking Joe what it felt like to knock someone out. "Different things at different times," Joe said. "I felt good knocking out Billy Conn, Max Schmeling, Max Baer and Carnera because there were so many people watching, and there was so much excitement. I mean, I was just coming up the ladder, and all these guys had been champions or big shots. It made me feel good knowing I could beat them. But knocking out a Johnny Paycheck or Al McCoy doesn't mean a thing to me."

It was all part of the game. Joe had to take the opponents as they came, some of them being not much more than sparring partners to keep him in shape for the tough ones. It was all part of maintaining the Heavyweight Champion's crown.

It was this same year, 1941, that Ted Jones, Joe's accountant, told him that he owed $81,000 in taxes. "Okay, pay it," Joe said.

Jones shook his head. "You don't understand how to work big finance. Don't pay them now; let it build up some more, then we can make a deal and settle for less."

Big finance! Joe knew nothing about that or tax laws. Jones was, after all, the accountant, supposedly knew what he was talking about. Joe went along with the scheme, and each year afterward his taxes seemed to double.

December 7, 1941, Joe relaxed with his family after a fine Thanksgiving reunion. They listened together as the radio announced that the Japanese had bombed Pearl Harbor. And later that same night came the announcement that America had officially declared war on Japan.

Soon afterward, Mike Jacobs called Joe at the Hillcrest Country Club in Los Angeles where he had been playing golf. Jacobs said he could get Joe a match to fight for the Navy Relief Fund, an organization that needed money badly. "I hope you understand, Joe, that you won't be getting paid for this one," Mike said over the phone.

"That's fine with me," Joe replied. He was angry over the attack on Pearl Harbor, the sneaky way the Japs had done it. If a fighter would have sneaked him like that, he would have busted the man's head. Fighting for the Navy Relief Fun was the least he could do.

Buddy Baer was chosen as his opponent. Buddy had fought a damn good fight in the first match, and seemed eager for a return bout. He agreed to donate one-sixth of his earnings to the Navy Relief Fund, and Joe agreed to donate all of his end of the gate, minus training expenses. The match was scheduled for January 9, 1942, at Madison Square Garden.

Joe's training for the second Buddy Baer fight was interrupted by an award. He had been chosen by the boxing writers' association of New York to receive the Edward J. Neil Trophy. It meant that Joe was the man who had done the most for boxing in the preceeding year.

At the weigh-in on January 9, Buddy Baer tipped the scales at 250 pounds, Joe at 205. The weight difference didn't bother Joe any until Chappie, in the dressing room just before the fight, said, "Joe, I can't make it in the corner with you tonight."

"But you *got* to!" Joe had never fought a professional fight without Chappie in his corner. The idea was unthinkable.

Sadly Chappie explained about the terrible pains of rheumatism and arthritis he was having, and that he didn't even know if he could get up the steps to the ring no less stay in Joe's corner.

"If you get up those stairs with me," Joe promised anxiouly, "I'll have Baer out before you can relax."

Chappie grinned his crooked grin. "Okay, Chappie. And remember, that's a promise."

Madison Square Garden looked like a patriotic rally. There were American flags flying everywhere. The war had brought the country together, and the charity match for the Navy Relief Fund had apparently reminded the fans of what the Japanese had done at Pearl Harbor.

Joe sat in his corner looking at the American flags—feeling good about what he was doing, feeling fine. But there was his promise to Chappie to keep. The trainer had made it up the stairs in visible pain, and Joe owed him more as a friend than as a business associate. The bell rang announcing round one. Joe gritted his teeth and reaffirmed the promise in his head. He shuffled forward in the style that had become famous by now, right hand cocked for the knockout.

Baer came out strong, managed a couple of left hooks. Bang! Joe blackened his left eye. Then a solid right to the chin, and Buddy Baer was down for a nine-count. Then up again, and immediately down again . . . another nine-count. Joe was there when he came off the canvas the second time . . . bang, *bang!* The referee stopped the fight because Baer's legs seemed to have turned to water.

Chappie's arthritis and rheumatism didn't hurt so bad after that promise was kept. The American government received $49,000 as Joe's share of the gate minus training expenses.

Three days after the Baer fight, Joe Louis volunteered for the Army. He knew he would be drafted, would have to serve anyway, but it was no spur-of-the-moment decision. He was still fighting mad over the way the Japanese had sneaked all those unsuspecting men at Pearl Harbor. Memories of the Schmeling rematch were stimulated, too: the Nazi propaganda machine that had painted him as something less than a human being. Enlisting was something he felt he had to do. He discussed it with his family, Marva, his managers and Mike Jacobs, and although he could have been declared exempt by claiming that Marva and his momma were dependent on him, the biggest fight of his life was being fought in both oceans and he wanted to be there.

Joe had come to the point in his career where he was tired of traveling and training, somewhat tired of fighting. It was an ugly war. When he had met Schmeling in the right, the political issues had been hazy, too much for a simple farm boy. Now he understood, because even Marva—sweet and pretty as she was—had experienced that kind of thing, at least to a degree, through the hotel incident in Bermuda. Black folks were fighting a similar battle every day on the streetb of big cities all over the United States. Marcus Garvey or no Marcus Garvey, he was an American and proud of it.

The Army offered Joe a commission when he arrived to enlist. "Ain't no way I can be no officer," he declined.

Joe was too simple a man to accept that kind of responsibility in war. He simply could not see himself telling a bunch of young guys to take some hill, and then have to live with the consequences of the decision.

"I want to be just a plain, ordinary G.I.," he told them. He was no leader, he knew.

Wartime. There were black boys barely old enough to shave being killed in defense of homeland and flag. That's what Joe wanted to be a part of—the fight. America had been good to him in spite of his blackness; he had managed to tear down some of the walls standing between his people and equality, and that was one of the issues being fought . . . white supremacy. There was a time in every man's life when he had to stand up for what he knew was right, and to hell with personal gain and risk to life. The flags flying at the Baer fight had triggered something inside him that had to be nurtured. Patriotism!

Joe was assigned to Camp Upton in Long Island, New York. He drove up in a chauffered-limousine, accompanied by Julian Black. He was issued his uniform and the rest of his plain G.I. ration. Then he was assigned to the "colored" section, along with the other black boys willing to die for their country.

16

Freddie Wilson was worried. Freddie was the friend Martha had called about Joe being in the room downstairs with Marie Johnson, and now it was the last day of January, 1969. Joe had refused to leave his suite in the Hotel Park Sheraton for the past two weeks. He had been visited there by Helen Dayton. A scene developed, and Joe had ripped off the woman's clothes. He then accused Miss Dayton of plotting against him, working with the Mafia to have him killed while he slept. Wilson called a Dr. Bennett in Detroit. "Can't do a thing with him," Wilson said. "He's blown his top. You'd better come out here."

Bennett had been Joe's physician for years. The doctor had been with Joe from one training camp to another almost since the beginning of the fighter's career. "Be there in the morning," he promised Wilson.

Louis seemed terrorized when Bennett arrived the next morning. He complained of pains all over his body, seemed hostile. Bennett was worried: Joe had always been so humble, appreciative of others. Now he seemed to hate people, even those closest to him. "Let me examine you, Joe," the doctor suggested.

"Naw!" Louis was gruff. He told the doctor about the Texan who had followed him into the suite to kill him—a fantasy. He was visibly having difficulty in breathing. Sweat dampened his clothes and dripped from his forehead. His hallucination kept returning to Miss Dayton as the prime mover in a hazy plot to kill him in his bed.

"I gotta get a blackjack or a pistol," Joe insisted. "I gotta protect myself." With a contorted face, he told how the walls were talking to him, and again about the Texan. Over and over again about the Texan, and how he needed to protect himself against such enemies.

"All right, Joe," Dr. Bennett cajoled. "You're going to be all right. You've got some wrestling shows to referee. Why don't you get going on that?"

Louis told about how he had tried to book plane reservations half a dozen times. Each time, at the last second, he had found it impossible to face the world outside the hotel room . . . those out there plotting his assassination.

Freddie Guinyard, who had accompanied Dr. Bennett from Detroit at Wilson's request, said, "Ain't nothing wrong with you, Joe. And there's nobody following you. Nobody wants to kill you. Hell, everybody loves you, Joe."

Silence from Louis, eyes darting.

"Look, Joe, you're coming out of this hotel," Dr.

Bennett added firmly.

"I ain't," Louis said.

"Well, let me tell you this," Bennett went on. "Your wife's on her way now. You can stay in and make a big scene, but Martha is on her way."

Joe's eyes went wide with the prospect. There had been too many big scenes with Martha lately, and the prospect seemed to frighten him even more than the delusions of assassins lying in wait outside the hotel room. Quickly he pulled on his clothes, picked up his overcoat, and said, "Goddamn, Freddie, pack my stuff and meet me downstairs."

"He was off in a second," Dr. Bennett revealed in *Brown Bomber,* published by *World Publishing Company,* 1972. "I used Martha's name to scare him. She wasn't coming in, but he was afraid of her then."

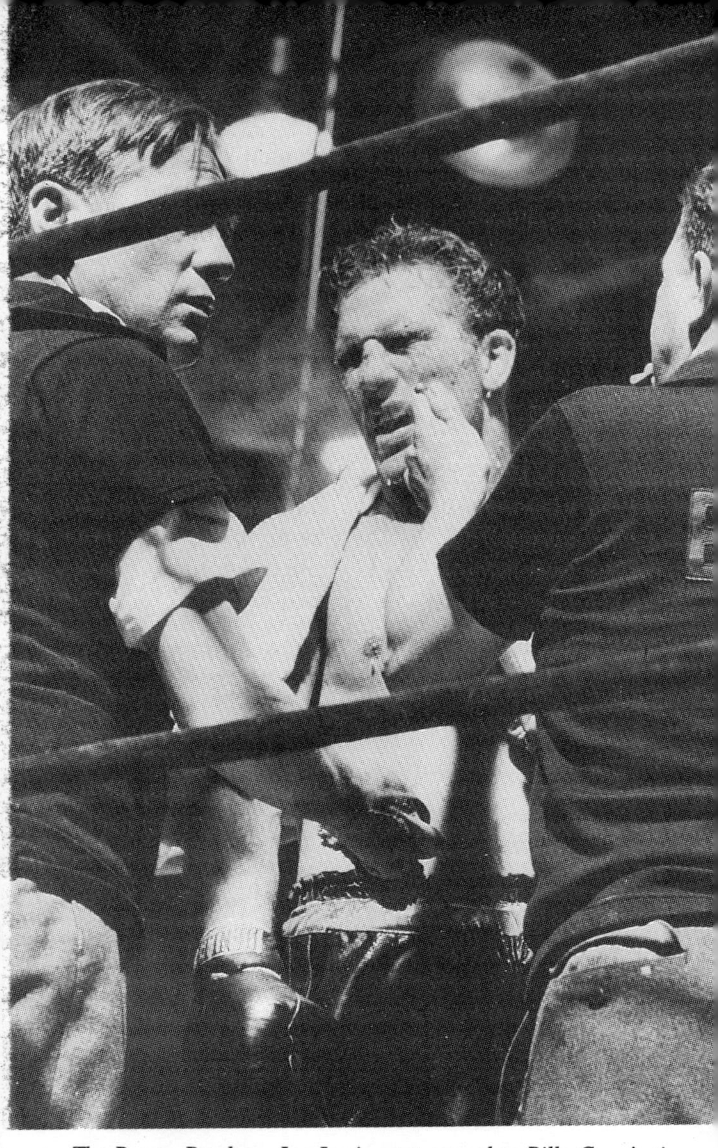

The Brown Bomber—Joe Louis—put an end to Billy Conn's ti-tle hopes on June 19, 1946, by knocking him out in the eighth round of their title bout at Yankee Stadium.

17

In 1942, 1969-70 was still a long ways away, and there was nothing like a good card game between Army buddies; nothing like little side bets and talk of women and some lies. Another benefit fight was coming up for Joe, this time for the Army Relief Fund—no paycheck for the man who was already getting in deeper with back taxes. This time it would be Abe Simon again, the man it had taken him thirteen rounds to get to in their first fight. The match was set for March 27 at Madison Square Garden.

Shortly before the fight, the Navy Relief Society asked Joe to be the guest speaker at one of their functions. The idea was spooky: Joe was not a public speaker, didn't know what to say. That, basically is what he said: "I'm only doing what any red-blooded American would do. We gonna do our part, and we will win, because we are on God's side."

In appreciation, President Roosevelt sent Joe a letter of contratulations.

At the benefit fight, the Undersecretary of War, Robert Patterson, and the Chairman of the War Production Board, Donald Nelson were in attendance. Both made speeches on Joe's generosity in contributing his share of the purse to the Army Relief Fund. The match was being broadcast by short wave to the boys overseas.

There was something missing, however: Chappie. Chappie was home in bed, really sick this time. The emptiness in the place where Chappie usually stood left an emptiness down deep in Joe. It was not the same without the gruff little man who had whispered and shouted strategy to Joe throughout his professional career.

Joe stared across the ring at the six-foot-four, 255-pound Abe Simon. He looked ready. Joe looked around at the 19,000 people in the spectator audience. Some of the poor black G.I.'s were there through tickets he himself had spent $3,000 on. The bell rang announcing round one.

Simon started the fight with a lot of inconsequential pokes that looked like a flurry. Joe brushed off the jabs. Not much happened until the fourth round when Joe got kind of tired of Simon's buzzing around like an agitated horsefly. Joe then let go with several hard rights and left hooks that opened a bad cut over Simon's right eye. Simon was almost out of his feet, groggy at the end of the fifth. Joe hit him with a right-left combination in the sixth and he was down for the count. This time Joe's donation to the American government was $75,000.

Chappie. Joe had really missed him in his corner. Now he was in the hospital with pneumonia. Joe immediately asked for a five-day furlough to be with his friend. What in the world would he ever do without Chappie?

But the hard little ex-fighter, ex-con, trainer extraordinaire was recovering. He looked older, thinner; but, Joe supposed, was just too contrary to give up the ghost over a little bout with pneumonia. They talked fights . . . most of the ones Joe had fought. Chappie had listened to the Simon match over the radio. He seemed pleased with the results. After all, it was him, good old Chappie, who had done most of the hard work in training Joe throughout the early stages of his career. Sometimes the Bomber's head had been harder than any punch either of them had taken throughout both career's combined.

They talked some about the Army. Joe was really getting an inside glimpse of what the war was all about—like a lot of the black G.I.'s he bunked with. Some were just little kids who had lied about their age to enlist, and what they needed most was to be back home with their mommas. For some, however, being in the Army was the best they had ever had it: three square meals a day, a bed of their own. Nazi Germany was the common motivator . . . black boys could relate very easily to what was happening to the Jews. What made Joe mad was the fact that some of them, those young kids, would never make it back alive and still they had to sleep in separate barracks, couldn't go to the same movies as the white guys and could hardly get into officer's training school. It was a kind of "move to the back of the bus" double standard that was not right at all.

Joe and Chappie discussed many things over that

five-day furlough, and there didn't seem to be a thing to worry about in that quarter when Joe returned to camp. Until the provost office said there was a telegram.

Joe got to the provost office as fast as he could, tore open the telegram. The words jumped out at him: "Chappie dead."

"My God," Joe whispered. His mind simply could not accept the thought. He kept reading the words over and over until they blurred with tears . . . Chappie dead . . . Chappie dead. Chappie had been his father, his teacher, a true friend. The loss was too great to endure: he cried openly, without shame or reservation, the words leaping from the telegram held in his big hands. Joe had never considered death. He had supposed, he knew now, that he would always be Heavyweight Champion, and that Chappie would always be right there in his corner.

The Army granted another furlough, two weeks this time, for Joe to attend the services, burial and whatnot. Chappie had died suddenly of a heart attack—unthinkable! There were at least 10,000 people at the Pilgrim Baptist Church where the services were held, more than the church could hold, and most of them standing outside in their mourning. Chappie was a true champion in his own right, and everyone seemed to know it.

It was a sad group of pallbearers—all of them stunned by the sudden loss—that carried the coffin from the hearse in Lincoln Cemetary: Joe and Roxy and Black, Cab Calloway, Bill Robinson and Carl Nelson. Together they watched as the box containing the remains of one of the best who had ever done it lowered into the harsh ground. it was still too incredible for Joe. Chappie's spirit would always be there at his side, whispering strategy between rounds and screaming from his corner when Joe slipped or refused to obey.

When the first handful of dirt was tossed into the grave after the coffin, Joe knew his life would never be the same.

November 11, 1952: Making his debut as a dancer at a New York nightclub, fighter Sugar Ray Robinson brought former champion Joe Louis to the stage for an introduction.

On Christmas Day, 1955, Joe Louis married businesswoman Rose Morgon but the marriage only lasted about six weeks. "I tried to make him settle down but I couldn't," she said later.

18

Joe was transferred to a cavalry division at Fort Riley, Kansas, after basic training. There he met Jackie Robinson. Racism ran rampant in the service, particularly in that part of the country, and soon after settling in, Jackie began to complain because he could not get on the camp baseball or football team. That made Joe angrier than most of the racial nonsense that was going on around him. He knew he had influence. He was raising a lot of money for the Army and Navy with his benefit fights—another one set for June 5 with George Nicholson, one of his former sparring partners at Fort Hamilton in Brooklyn—and so he went to Brigadier General Donald Robinson and asked about why there was a racial discrimination in ballplaying in that camp.

"Don't you know you've got one of the outstanding football players in the country in this camp?" Joe demanded.

"Who are you talking about?" Brigadier General Robinson wanted to know.

"Jackie Robinson from UCLA." If there was any man in the world Joe would have liked to have been like, it was Jackie. And the sentiment was reversed on Jackie's part.

The general apologized, said he had not been aware of any such situation. Of course he wanted Robinson and any other *qualified* Negroes to play on the team. He would have it no other way, make no mistake about it. Joe hurried back to tell Jackie.

"I'm not playing no football unless they let me play baseball, too," a stubborn Robinson said.

Back to the General for Joe, and then back to Jackie with another approval. As it turned out, Jackie Robinson—ironic that he was the General's namesake—wound up the champion baseball and football player at Fort Riley. More important, it opened the racial lines in other parts of the country for integrated ball playing at Army Camps. It seemed that black folks were fighting a war of their own inside the war that was threatening most of the civilized world. Ironic that the American Army was battling Hitler's racist philosophies, yet practicing some of them, too.

Marva was pregnant, and Joe had been promoted from corporal to sargeant. The Army felt that he could best serve his country as a moral booster, and through refereeing exhibition fights all over the states. Okay by Joe, but with one strong stipulation—he absolutely refused to appear anywhere to segregated Army groups, and that was final.

One small victory, one major defeat: the Army had turned down Jackie Robinson's application for Officer's Candidate School. Seventeen other black enlisted men had been turned down, too. Another visit for Joe to the Brigadier General's office, but with unsatisfactory results this time. Joe Louis was pissed! The public image of the quiet, shy Louis was overrun by his determination to do something about what the Army was doing to college-educated black boys. He put through a call to Truman Gibson, Jr., a black serving in the War Department.

An investigation was launched by Gibson on Joe's accusation. As a result, fifteen black men, including Jackie Robinson, were accepted into Officer's Candidate School. Joe was proud of himself, even more when Jackie graduated a lieutenant. Minor battles were being won at the homefront to compensate for the Black youngsters being shot up and killed by the racist soldiers halfway around the world.

Billy Conn had joined the Army shortly after Joe, and now Mike Jacobs had arranged for the two to meet in a rematch for the Army Relief Fund. Thing was, though, Joe owed Mike Jacobs $59,000, and another $41,000 to Roxborough. Billy owed Jacobs an additional $30,000. It was a lot of money, but not so very much when one considered that the Army was expecting a million-dollar gate from the scheduled rematch.

Mike Jacobs did what seemed fair: he sat down for a powwow with the Army committee in charge of the fight, outlined the financial status of both Louis and Conn. the special committee agreed that the law stating that no one should get payments for private purposes while serving in the Armed Forces could be revised in this case so that both fighters could meet their financial obligations: a nice twist, until Secretary of War Stimson canceled the fight because he was upset by the money arrangements. Both Louis and Conn were ordered back to camp from their training camps . . . this, after Joe had donated well over $100,000 through previous charity matches, and an untold amount of money through the fund raising campaigns. The Army sure had its own way of doing things.

Joe was shocked, happy and acting foolish when he received the news that Marva had given birth to a baby girl. Months before, he had set up a place for her near the camp. But it was too hot and sticky in Kansas, and soon she had returned home to be near her family and friends. Now Joe was scheduled to go to Hollywood to play a role in the movie *This is The Army*. It seemed they were fated to be apart at the most crucial times.

The baby was named Jacqueline. Joe was granted a week's furlough before he had to be in Hollywood as a "morale" builder for the boys overseas.

Irony following irony, Joe was called to Washington to sit with members of the War Department on a proposed overseas tour for American soldiers. That seemed like a fine idea to Joe: it was January, 1944, the movie *This is The Army* completed after six months, was followed by a 100-day tour around the country setting up exhibition bouts. It seemed fine to Joe until, at Camp Silbert, Alabama, he and Sugar Ray Robinson sat on a bench at the post bus station . . . *Joe Louis and Sugar Ray Robinson were told by a white M.P. that they would have to move to the colored section.*

"We ain't moving," Joe growled.

"Well, then, you're under arrest," the M.P. said.

At the provost marshall's office, Joe was told that he

was a soldier and had to do what an M.P. said, no matter who he happened to be otherwise.

"Listen," Joe said. "I'm an American. I'll go along with the Jim Crow laws in town, but I don't see any reason why I have to sit in the back of an Army bus station."

The provost marshall continued to preach about soldiers being under an obligation to do whatever an M.P. said, no matter who they happened to be in personal life. There would be no exceptions to Army regulations.

"Let me call Washington," Joe said.

The provost marshall's attitude changed immediately: a discrepency, Joe and Sugar Ray were free to go. Word travels fast along the Army grapevine; and soon after the incident, an *order* was issued from Higher Command. There were to be no more Jim Crow busses in Army Camps.

Different type of wars were being waged on all fronts, it seemed: Roxy had been arrested in Detroit for running a numbers racket, and Richard Reading, the former mayor, was being charged with conspiring to protect the operation. Joe was off on his European morale tour for the Army. Roxy, the man who had put so many poor black kids through college with part of the money he'd made from the numbers, was being sentenced to two-to-five. Ultimately, he served two and one-half years.

The European tour included fights in England, Italy and Africa. The world was topsy-turvy . . . the war . . . Chappie gone . . . Roxy in prison. There was no stability anywhere, it seemed. At home there was Marva and baby Jacqueline. Joe, in a bomber, headed for London with Billy Conn at his side.

"Joe, why couldn't you have let me hold the title for six months? I would have given it back," Billy said.

Joe laughed. He remembered how Conn had "hit and run" throughout the first twelve rounds. "Billy, you had the title for twelve rounds and you couldn't hold it. How in hell were you going to hold it for six months?"

They both laughed: topsy-turvy. The landing gear on the bomber was stuck, and they circled the field . . . around and around and around for forty-five minutes. Poor Chappie. The exchange had made Joe remember that the gruff little ex-con was not in his corner now, and that Roxy was sitting somewhere back in the states in a cell.

His own private war was about to begin again with Marva. This time there would be no reconciliation; no time for him to get it together and prove himself to her. There just seemed to be no stability anywhere in life.

19

At last the war was over, America victorious. Joe Louis was thirty-two. He had been in ninety-six exhibition fights, had traveled over 70,000 miles and was seen by over 5,000,000 servicemen. Now he had his own career to see to: his life. There were exorbitant amounts of money owed. A stretch of canvas, surrounded by ropes, was the only means he had of making things good for himself once more. His discharge included the Legion of Merit Medal for exceptionally meritorious conduct. He was a civilian again as of October 1, 1945.

Mike Jacobs was quick to act. Billy Conn was to be Joe's next opponent with the match set for June 19, 1946, at Yankee Stadium. Joe was in debt to Jacobs for $100,000.

Good things started to happen again: Joe read in the papers that his Army buddy, Jackie Robinson, had been hired by the Brooklyn Dodgers' Montreal Royals farm club in the International League. Jackie was to be the first Negro to play in modern organized baseball. Robinson would set records for baseball ability and high earnings.

For Joe, 1945-46, finances were so bad that he went to Black for a loan against future fight purses. Black insisted he had no money to spare . . . a lie, Joe knew. Angry, Joe reminded Black of the contract that gave him 25 percent of the fighter for ten years. The ten-year period was up. Joe signed the twenty-five percent over to Marva—better than paying alimony—naming her as a co-manager. Then, with Roxborough's approval, Joe signed on Marshall Miles of Buffalo to take Black's place as manager.

Uncle Sam was waiting in line along with the other bill collectors with his back-taxes statement in the amount of $81,000. Cash was needed. An old friend, Billy Rowe, seemed to be the answer. Billy wanted to open a black public relations and advertising agency. It sounded odd to Joe. He had never heard of a black public relations firm. But Bill said that was the point. He had done some research, learned that black people in Harlem alone, were gambling away almost a quarter of a million dollars a day. Billy felt certain that if they opened a black public relations agency, they could convince big business to cater more to black people, not out of goodness, but rather for the money to be made. His theory was that black people would buy more of a certain product if they saw black models, and since Joe was a big name all over the world, Billy thought sure corporate executives would buy the scheme. Billy Rowe was no dummy. He had been Deputy Police Commissioner in New York and had worked as a columnist on the *Pittsburg Courier*.

It all sounded great to Joe. Billy was well-known in Harlem, and there were, in fact, no black models at the time . . . except maybe for good old Aunt Jemima on the Farina box. The first job, of course, was to publicize the Louis-Conn fight. Jacobs had managed to get the price for ringside seats at $100 a ticket.

Between exhibition fights, Joe still saw Marva. They developed a sort of live-together, not live-together arrangement that seemed to work. She was there when Joe needed her, and the baby was growing, a part of both of them that they willingly shared.

The Pompton Lakes training camp looked good after all that time away. Joe had fought ten exhibition fights in November and December of 1945, but now he had to prepare for the real thing. Conn was no pushover, he recalled. Plus he was no longer the twenty-seven-year-old who had gone against the competent Billy the first time around. Now he, Louis, was thirty-two, Billy Conn a vigorous twenty-four. It would not be easy.

Chappie was gone. Mannie Seamon had taken his place as Joe's training, and now proceeded to line up the biggest and toughest sparring partners he could find. But it was no good . . . Joe remained slow, out of shape. Reporters who watched the training sessions began to print bad write-ups about Joe, and to laude the way Conn was training himself into peak condition. Still, Joe remained confident.

At the weigh-in, Joe looked long and hard at Billy Conn. He had gained about fifteen pounds in four years, was not the same man who had almost taken the title. He looked good, looked fine. But Joe knew he could not be as fast as he was with the extra weight on. There would be no ballet this time, maybe a slugout, and nobody, but nobody, had ever beaten the Brown Bomber toe-to-toe.

The first disappointment came in the gate for the fight. Jacobs had expected at least $3,000,000. Instead it was $2,000,000. Still, it was the second biggest gate in boxing history, the rematch between Tunney and Dempsey holding the record. There would be more than enough in the winner's share to pay the back taxes and catch up on those other big debts, Joe knew. All he had to do was get out there and win.

When the bell for round one rang, both Joe and Billy came out and began to spar—a warm up. Billy said, "Take it easy, Joe, we've got fifteen rounds to go."

Joe laughed. They were friends now, war buddies, and that made a difference. The fight became a comedy . . . Billy jumping around like a dancer, Joe waiting for him to come in. The crowd booed. They had paid a lot of money to see a fight, and what they were seeing was anything but that. Both fighters had been away from the professional ring for what might be too long a time. Joe was still confident, however. He knew by the third round that he would have to go after Conn to win the fight.

For the next four rounds, until the seventh, Joe kept shuffling forward, pressing Conn. Conn back-pedaled. He was no longer the prima donna he had been, but his movements remained sure and quick.

Instead of Chappie being there to tell Joe what to do, Joe told Marshall Miles and Mannie Seamon that he was going to go out and slug to see if Billy could really take it in round eight. He was the Champion, he knew. The bell rang. He went out hard and immediately opened a cut beneath Conn's left eye. Next Conn's knees buckled from a strong right to the chin. Then Joe threw a left hook and a right cross, and Billy was flat on his back on the canvas. The referee counted him out in two minutes and nineteen seconds of the eighth round. Chappie had been there in spirit after all.

It was an easy enough fight, much easier than Joe's first run-in with Billy Conn. But it was a bad showing. Another rematch was called for, and Joe wanted that to happen as quickly as possible. Pride demanded it.

Joe's share of the gate? Close to $625,000. Half of that went to Marva, Roxborough and Marshall. Uncle Sam got the $81,000 owed from the first Billy Conn fight, and Mike Jacobs got the $100,000 due him. Another $25,000 went to Billy Rowe to officially open the black public relations firm. By the time Joe's bills were paid, he was near broke again.

More confusion and heartbreak. Isaac Woodard, a black veteran, had been attacked by Southern policemen who poked both his eyes out with their nightsticks. A committee was formed to stage a benefit for Woodard, and Joe was asked to appear. "Nobody in America should have to go through second class citizenship," he told the gathering. "Me and a whole lot of black guys went out fighting for the American cause, now we're gonna have to get America to give us our civil rights, too. We earned them." The speech had not been prepared, it just flowed. The policemen who had attacked Woodard had done so without apparent reason. Joe was sick of it—sick of the racism and bigotry that black boys had fought against in Europe and the Philippines and died because of it. Hitler had been white. The policemen who attacked Woodard were white also, and suffered from a variation of the same disease. The war was over across the big water, and already there were plans to lend assistance in rebuilding the enemy nations. Yet here in the states, against guys like Woodard who had fought valiantly, the endless war of discrimination was still being waged.

More confusion, and hate. Ring politics. Fixes. Harry Mendel came to see him. Harry was a fight publicist. He told Joe that "some people" had a proposition concerning "some fighter," and they would hand over one million dollars if the Brown Bomber would do business. They were willing to meet Joe on the Staten Island Ferry, atop the Empire State Building, wherever he chose to do business. A million dollars tax free was his for the taking.

Joe laughed at Mendel. "Ain't that some hot shit." He could see Chappie's ghost coming back to whup his black ass.

"My profession is boxing and my title is Champion," he would say of the incident years later in his autobiography. "Got too much pride in myself and my people to mess that up for anything or anybody."

September 18 brought Tami Mauriello at Yankee Stadium. Tami was a big guy from the Bronx. He could punch like a mule, but he wasn't much of a boxer. Joe did not consider him any great threat when they stepped through the ropes into the ring. Again he was surprised: Tami hit him with a right to the chin that almost put Joe down in the first round. But instead of moving in when the Bomber was hurt, finishing the job, Mauriello eased up. Then Joe's famous combinations flew, and Tami, not the Brown Bomber, was down. He came up after a five-count and Joe dropped him again. Again he came up—game, but . . . ! Joe flurried on him, and Referee Donovan counted him out in round one.

Joe was feeling good again, looking fine. The match was over almost before it had begun, so fast that Joe didn't even have to take a shower afterward.

More debts were paid with the purse, and more bouts were fought in Honolulu and Mexicali, Mexico. Another $90,000 and most of it disappeared almost overnight.

Next Mike Jacobs arranged a tour for the winter of 1947 in Central and South America. Arturo Godoy was to be the first opponent on the exhibition tour, a scheduled ten-rounder. Joe was surprised by the cheers he got—more than Godoy. He, Joe, had remained undefeated Champion for one hell of a long time.

Irony upon irony, after so many years of marriage and only one child, now divorced, Marva gave birth to Joe Louis Barrow, Jr., on May 24, 1947 . . . the son Joe had always dreamed of fathering. Later the boy would come to be known affectionately as "Punchie."

There were more inconsequential exhibition bouts through San Diego, Spokane and Los Angeles. Still, no one happened to be around for a bona-fide championship bout. No one except Joe Baksi who refused a contract with Joe to fight Olle Tandberg, a Swedish heavyweight of some acclaim.

Jacobs came up with the idea of another exhibition fight with a black guy named Arnold Cream, better known as Jersey Joe Walcott. He had been one of Louis' sparring partners in preparation for the first Schmeling fight and was good. The catch came when the New York State Athletic Commission said "no" to a ten-round exhibition fight. They said exhibition bouts went only six rounds, and a ten-rounder had to be a championship match. Of course, Joe said okay: what was there to worry about anyway?

In November Joe trained for the December 5 match. But there was something missing now . . . Chappie? Old age creeping up as it does on athletes? Whatever it was,

Joe no longer enjoyed getting up before dawn for road-work, faking out sparring partners. He was 218 pounds—too heavy. Taking off weight was much more of a chore now than it had ever been, no fun at all. The kick seemed to have gone out of the whole thing, and secretly, silently, the great Joe Louis Barrow as considering retirement.

Joe came in at 211 pounds on the day of the weigh-in. He had hardly eaten a thing, hardly sipped water for days. He remembered the first match with Billy Conn when Chappie had screamed because he went on such a diet to get his weight down—a replay? It had been a long time between professional fights, too. Everything seemed to be stacked against Joe when he stepped into the ring at Madison Square Garden that night, and faced Jersey Joe Walcott . . . a man who had once been his sparring partner and had stormed out of the Pompton Lakes camp one day when Joe hurt him.

The bell rang and Walcott came forward. He laid into Joe with a series of left jabs and hooks to open the fight. Joe pressed forward. Walcott stopped dancing, landed a solid right to the jaw that sent the Champion to the canvas. Was it actually happening, the roar of the crowd seemed to ask? Was the mighty Joe Louis about to succumb?

Joe was up at the count of two. Enraged, he attacked without thinking, without style. Walcott danced back out of reach of the frantic lefts and rights thrown so wildly by the Champion. Walcott continued to dance through the second and third rounds while Joe's anger made him flail at the air in front of the man.

Less than one minute into round four, Walcott landed a right to the Champion's jaw that made Louis' knees buckle. Joe stayed on his hands and knees while the referee counted to seven. It was hard to believe, from that vantage point, that he, Joe Louis, was the twenty-to-one favorite . . . ears ringing . . . eyes somewhat glazed. He clinched with Walcott: desperation. Jersey Joe shook him loose, and proceeded to scientifically beat the Champion punchy.

Nothing much happened in the next four rounds: Louis pressed, Jersey Joe back-pedaled. In the ninth Louis landed a hard right that was just a bit too high to do the knockout damage intended. Jersey Joe was against the ropes now, Louis pouring lefts and hard rights into his head and body. Later, Joe would admit that he thought he had Walcott at that point. But when the round ended and Walcott was still standing, Joe knew he had lost his one and only hope of a knockout.

Walcott was a black Bob Pastor for the rest of the night, determined to go the distance: fifteen rounds. He maintained his back-pedaling, fought in spurts. He wasn't coming to him, Joe kept thinking as the last rounds progressed. He, Walcott, had to come to the Champion to win it on points . . . at least that was the way it was supposed to be.

When it was finally over, the bell announcing the end of round fifteen having sounded, Joe wanted nothing more than to get out of the ring. He was disgusted with himself, the way he had fought the match. The decision made it worse . . . Judge Marty Monroe, nine to six in favor of Louis . . . Judge Frank Forbes, eight to six, one even, in favor of Louis . . . Referee Ruby Goldstein, seven to six, two even, in favor of Louis.

Indeed, Joe had won. But the crowd booed the decision, and the usual feeling of victory after a well-fought bout was not present in the Champion. All he could think of now was that he would have to fight Walcott again—and soon—to get rid of the bad taste in his own mouth, and to erase all doubt from the minds of the fans who had booed him.

To make things worse, letters and telegrams began pouring in to the New York Athletic Commission within the next two days that claimed Joe Louis should not have been given the decision. The newspapers, the governor of New York and the mayor of the city received like complaints. It was the first time in the Brown Bomber's career that the fans had turned against him. The fact penetrated deep inside Joe like the boos he had heard when he stepped from the ring. It left him with a sense of depression that he had not felt since he received the telegram saying Chappie was dead.

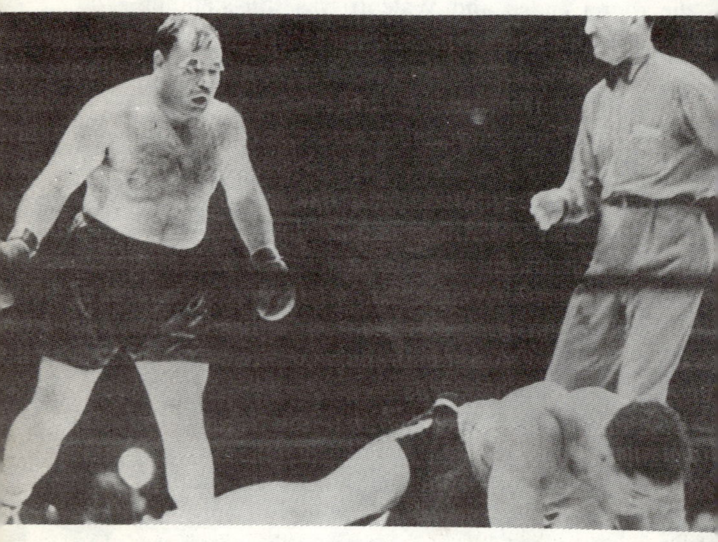

When Champion Joe Louis met Tony Galento at Yankee Stadium on June 28, 1939, the championship belt was on the line and it appeared that Louis was in trouble early on. He won by a knockout, however, in the fourth round.

20

Taxes again. Joe owed the government $196,000 from 1946, and here it was '48. He was still broke. He had dreamed of retiring as Champion. Now . . . ?

There was an exhibition match with Bob Foxworth slated for Chicago on January 29. Joe wanted the rematch with Walcott. Whatever else happened to him, wherever he ended and when, he had to get back in the ring with Jersey Joe to silence those boos that seemed to ring loud in his head whenever he recalled the night of their first fight.

Jersey Joe. At least Louis was defending his title to another black man, the second such contender in his career. The match was set for June 25 at Yankee Stadium. It was a good crowd and good money. Joe needed the money because the tax people were sniffing around him again, claiming he had borrowed large sums from businesses he owned and had not paid any taxes on such. The tax people were always there now, it seemed . . . digging . . . finding more money owed. The gate from the Bob Foxworth fight had not even dented his outstanding debt to Uncle Sam.

The bell rang. Louis stepped out cautiously this time. This time, he had promised himself, he would not fight Jersey Joe's fight. Rather he would force the contender to come in and play his game. Jersey Joe seemed to know as much, too: knew that if the Champion caught him, he was dead. The result was that nothing much happened, except the crowd booed again, for the first nine rounds. In the tenth, Referee Frank Fullam shouted, "Hey, one of you get the lead out of your ass, and let's have a fight." It irked Louis. Nobody had ever before had to tell him to get in there and *fight* before . . . more boos from the crowd.

Jersey Joe was beginning to look tired in the eleventh, and Louis went after him, giving it everything he had. And then it happened: Jersey Joe made the same mistake—overconfidence—that Billy Conn had made. Louis hit him with a devastating right to the chin, followed by three hard lefts to the head. Walcott's legs gave out. His hands dropped and his eyes rolled. He fell and was counted out in two minutes and fifty-six seconds of the eleventh round.

There were no boos this time. It was old times all over again, with the thrill of victory taking the place of the deep down depression Joe had felt after his first match with Joe from Jersey. Jolting Joe Louis was still the Brown Bomber Champion the fans had cheered throughout his professional career. It was a good feeling.

One victory, and one defeat. Joe had promised Marva that he would retire and now he was telling her to pack her bags for a tour that would last from September through December. No way, not for Marva, not again. It was fine when she was younger, she said, when there were no children to think of—only her and Joe. This time she simply was not going, and that was that. "Your timing is off, Joe," Marva said. "And your timing for marriage was off, too."

There was no answer for that, not in Joe. This time it seemed to be final.

Joe buried himself in work with poor black kids to forget, and buried in bouts that took him from Nashville to Boston, Cleveland, Detroit, St. Louis, Oklahoma City and more. He fought over twenty bouts before Christmas of 1948, including another decision over his friend and Army buddy, Billy Conn. Then Joe took a short break for the holidays before the next series of exhibitions began on January 10, 1949.

Mike Jacobs came down sick in January, and Joe went to see him. They spent a long time trying to cheer each other up—two old pros getting past the stage where they should have retired. Joe went back to his hotel suite on the South Side of Miami to think for a while alone after their chat. He stared out the window. This was the section of Miami where colored folks were "allowed" to live . . . Jesus Christ! Mike Jacobs was finished, would never be back, Joe knew. Mike simply didn't have the gumption any more.

"And neither do I," Joe thought aloud. He knew that. He was tired and needed a new way to make some big money.

The idea to form a boxing club of his own struck Joe suddenly. He thought about the Chicago Stadium owned by Jim Norris. Norris seemed to own a piece of just about everything in sports in the U.S. He had the Detroit Red Wings and the Chicago Black Hawks hockey clubs, the Chicago Stadium and it was rumored that he was ready to move in on Madison Square Garden now that Jacobs was ailing. There was nothing to lose in approaching Norris, and everything to be gained if he liked the idea.

Joe's proposition to Norris was that as the "retired" Heavyweight Champion he could name the two men who would fight it out for the title. Norris was interested, wanted to talk more about it. There was hardly time between the exhibition bouts stretching out ahead of Joe, but he was to be in the Chicago area in March. He promised Norris he would stop by to discuss the deal further.

More bouts, more purses pumped into debts, Chicago and the promised talk with Jim Norris and Arthur Wirtz, an associate: Joe revealed his idea of naming Jersey Joe Walcott and Ezzard Charles as the two contenders for the Heavyweight Championship once he retired. Joe told Norris he wanted $250,000 for getting the match together. Norris went him one better . . . $300,000 if he could arrange the match, a salary of $20,000 a year, and the vice presidency of their new corporation, the International Boxing Club.

It sounded good, sounded fine. Joe knew they would be competing with the Twentieth Century Sporting Club, Mike Jacob's organization, but it didn't seem to matter with Mike no longer there. Joe had paid plenty of dues to Twentieth Century, had made them millions. Joe hired Truman Gibson to work with him because he was still signed up for exhibition bouts for the rest of March, and they got the Jersey Joe Walcott/Ezzard Charles fight set to go for June 22.

The exhibition tour took Joe through Cuba and Texas, and ended in Washington, D.C. From there he went to New York to see Billy Rowe. They were still partners in the public relations thing, and now Joe did a few public appearances for Billy to help the business go. Then it was back to Chicago Stadium to see who would be the next Heavyweight Champion of the World.

It was not Joe's idea of an exciting fight. As a matter of plain fact, it wasn't *anyone's* idea of an exciting championship bout. Charles won the fifteen-round decision, but he looked dull. He worked like a bona-fide scientist in the ring, however, and even the N.B.A. thought the title had fallen into good hands. The New York Boxing Commission objected: it was their opinion that Charles should not hold the crown. They felt that there should have been more elimination fights with some of the foreign talent included.

Other champions had done what Joe had done, and now there was an objection. Jim Jeffries had done it without static. Was it because Joe was black and the others had been white that the New York Boxing Commission was balking? Or was it that they simply did not want another black champion?

Joe forgot the objections to concentrate on business—and *to hell* with the New York Boxing Commission! They signed Charles to fight Gus Lesnevich in New York in August. It was the first time a black heavyweight champion was being brought forward into the big time by a black promoter—Joe Louis. Mike Jacobs had taught him well. He knew all the pitfalls. What he hadn't figured on though was the harassment Charles would receive because people around the boxing game were saying that the only way he could really be recognized as the titleholder was to fight and beat Joe Louis.

No way, Joe thought. He was too old and had too many other more important things to do. He was finished with boxing. At least he was finished with boxing for the time being.

Charles stopped Gus Lesnevich in seven, a good fight. Next he went against Pat Valentino on October 14 in San Francisco. He was a good boy and coming along, looking good, looking fine.

Joe was on exhibition tour again from October through December. It was not to the ex-champion's liking, but Uncle Sam was breathing hot down his neck for those back taxes.

Joe finished 1949 doing exhibitions, and Ezzard Charles knocked Pat Valentino out in eight rounds— Joe Louis, the promoter. He had made a killing there, and another $300,000 off the exhibition tours throughout the year. Plus there were his investments and companies. But the more he made, the more seemed to go to hazy sources. His lawyers and the tax people knew. They had told him that he owed the government $50,000 a year in interest and penalties, and that had nothing to do with the principle tax of over a quarter of a million dollars. It was becoming a vicious circle. Joe had to keep working to make money to pay off the tax debt, and the more he worked, the more he owed and the less he had.

21

The new year brought even more tax problems for Joe. It began as a swell idea: a soft drink called the Joe Louis Punch. Al Lockhart, the black public relations man who had thought of it, a friend of Joe's, got it off the ground in January, and it was a dead horse by April. Joe fought twenty-three exhibition matches in that period, still trying to catch up on all those back taxes the government and his lawyers said he owed. Then *bang!* Another knockout by Uncle. The government had filed another tax lien, $59,000 this time, against Joe on the Joe Louis Punch deal that had folded. They froze any money he might get from his properties. Nor would they allow him expense money for training camp, or to cash in the settlements he had given to Marva after each fight. It was like having the plague. Once you get it, you're dead. It seemed to Joe that he was single-handedly supporting the United States government tax bureau.

Golf seemed to be the only thing that could take his mind off the debts he owed these days. It relaxed him, made him feel whole again. Even this was shattered when, playing a course in Los Angeles, someone came running up to him with a newspaper. Joe read in dismay the item about Marva having married Dr. Albert Spaulding on May 21, 1950. Joe's world was coming apart faster than he could cope. He remembered something the tax people had said when they told him he could not cash in on the settlements he had given to Marva after each fight. It had made no sense to him then, but now it did. The tax people had said he could not cash in on the settlements because of something in the *remarriage* laws complicating things.

There was nothing left for Joe Louis to do except announced that he had decided to come out of retirement to go against Ezzard Charles for the Heavyweight Championship. With everything else gone, it was the one thing he had left. He would be the first retired champion to ever regain the title.

22

Joe had not fought professionally in two years, and there were only six weeks to prepare to meet Ezzard Charles. The IBC wanted the fight to go off in September at Yankee Stadium. Joe wanted it held at the Garden in December—more time to prepare. Jim Norris insisted. There was just not enough time to prepare, and the Brown Bomber knew it.

He knew it even more on September 27 as he sat in his dressing room before the fight. He was thirty-six years old, weighed 218. Charles was twenty-nine and weighed in at 183½ pounds. His opponent would be fast, Joe knew. But he figured the extra weight might give him the edge needed. Either way, Uncle Sam wanted his money, and Joe had to live, too.

The fight started with Charles jabbing and punching Joe all over the ring, a pathetic sight for fight fans who had followed the Bomber's career. The younger, faster, lighter man simply wore the ex-champion out, cut him up. Joe reflects: "He hooked, jabbed, and got some good lefts to my stomach. When he started the crosses to my face, I dazed some. When I saw an opening, I couldn't get to it fast enough. My reflexes were rusted and my coordination was messed up."

After the fifth round, Sugar Ray Robinson, at ringside with Acting Mayor Vincent Impellitteri, came up the aisle to tell Joe's handlers, "Joe's got to keep sticking with that left hand. He's got to take the play away from Charles and keep him off balance."

The advice did no good. By the end of the seventh round, Joe knew he had bought it. He was too old, too tired. Too many professional fights, and too many back taxes. He was bleeding all over the ring by the end of the fourteenth, and Mannie Seamon and Marshall Miles practically had to lift him off the stool to answer the bell for the fifteenth. No contest. Charles retained the title.

Joe called his Momma after the fight. She begged him to stop now, give up boxing. Momma didn't understand about the tax people. Not even Joe did. All he knew was that they were there, wherever he went. They were there and they wanted their money. Fighting was the only way he knew how to get it.

It was 1951, and there was a string of fighters standing between Joe and a rematch with Ezzard Charles. The first was Freddie Beshore in Detroit on January 3: a knockout for Louis in four rounds.

Next was Cuban heavyweight Omelio Agramonte in Miami and another victory for Louis in ten rounds. A rematch with Agramonte ended the same way: decision to Louis after ten rounds. Then Joe got a match with Lee Savold, who held the British Empire heavyweight title. Another knockout for Louis, this time in six rounds, and well on his way back to the top of the heap.

Marciano was coming up—thirty-seven fights and thirty-two knockouts. He was a tough boy, looked like a contender. Jim Norris smelled money if Rocky and Joe went at it, a powerhouse gate. He offered Joe a guaranteed $300,000 to sign the contract.

On October 26, 1951, when the two fighters climbed through the ropes in Madison Square Garden, Joe was confident of victory. Marciano was a street brawler, and the ex-champion had handled man of them. The bell rang and Joe proceeded to box the 27-year-old Marciano all over the ring . . . feeling good, looking fine. And it remained that way until the seventh round.

Suddenly Joe's legs gave out. He had to be lifted off the stool to answer the bell for round eight. Marciano knocked him down almost immediately with a left hook. Joe stayed on the canvas for an eight-count, managed to drag himself upright. Marciano caught him with another left that sent the Brown Bomber crashing into the ropes, followed this with a looping right hand. The punch hit Joe in the neck and he fell through the ropes. Joe lay spent and dazed, his head against the ring apron and just his legs still inside the ring. He was too groggy to hear Referee Ruby Goldstein stop the fight.

Another exhibition tour followed—Joe's last. This time it was the Far East. November and December spent. At the end of the tour, Joe realized that he had netted only $20,000 and that the tax boys would be waiting for him back in the states.

Ezzard Charles, Marciano, all had failed. Horses and soda pop named after him, and a black public relations firm. What was left? Where did a man who knew nothing but fighting go in the end? Was there a graveyard like the elephants are supposed to have where ex-champions go to lie down and die?

Joe looked at himself in a mirror and wondered what in hell he was going to do.

In his later years "The Champ" became a celebrity attraction at Las Vegas' Caesar's Palace. Here he gives a New York vistor a few pointers on playing the slots.

23

Joe Louis had accumulated a record of seventy-one fights in his professional career. Of these, fifty-four ended by knockouts, sixty-eight wins, and three defeats. Impressive! Also impressive was the fact that the Brown Bomber defended his Heavyweight Championship twenty-five times and held the title for twelve years. His earnings were five million dollars, and he ended by owing the government one million. A career full of applause, cheering crowds, lots of victories and some defeats.

Then Momma died. Her estate was to be divided between the family. Joe's share was $660. The tax people took it.

Joe had to move on, do something to occupy the

troubled spot in his mind. He went to New York and the Louis-Rowe agency. It was not much, not nearly what he was used to, but it kept the aging ex-champion busy and paid his expenses.

And then the *coup de grace* from the tax people. They confiscated the annuities Marva had so carefully put aside for the children—more hurt for Joe's head. Now there seemed to be hurt wherever he turned.

Little lights in the dark: *Ring Magazine* included Joe Louis in the Boxing Hall of Fame in October, 1954. Now, at least, his name would remain as immortal as Jack Dempsey and Henry Armstrong. Perhaps in a hundred years or so when he was gone, a small black kid, thumbing through the pages of an old magazine, would be prompted to do something great because Joe had existed.

A second marriage. Impulsive. Christmas Day, 1955. Rose Morgan Louis, the ceremony held at her beautiful house in St. Albans, Long Island. The old-timers were there on behalf of Joe and the bride: Count Basie, Roy Campanella, baby-sister Vunice and Freddie Guinyard. Next morning just about every paper in the country ran the story. Jolting Joe Louis was in the headlines again.

Soon after, Ray Tabani, a professional wrestling promoter, offered $100,000 guaranteed if Joe would wrestle. Joe accepted immediately . . . money! His new wife was upset. "It's like seeing President Eisenhower wash dishes," she said.

Joe ignored her, just as he had overlooked Marva's wishes throughout their troubled marriage. His first match was in March. He won. It felt good to Joe to be a winner again, and to have some money in his pocket to spend on good times. There had been so very few good times lately.

Then refereeing was added to the wrestling, and boxing, too. Now Joe began to appear in one capacity or another two and three times a week. Things were looking good again, looking just fine, until a 340-pound wrestler named Cowboy Rocky Lee accidently stepped on Joe's chest when he was down, and the cracked ribs damaged some heart muscles. There would be no more wrestling for Joe Louis, no way.

But Joe Louis was not forgotten. A lot of people all over the country knew of his tax problem and wanted to help. In Norfolk, Nebraska, George Reeves, President of a pipeline company and a mortician, got together with John Youngheim, a commercial pilot, to organize a group of businessmen and set up a charter fund to help Joe out of his problems with Uncle Sam. Jack Dempsey was the Honorary Chairman. They helped as best they could, going so far as trying to talk to the government about a "reasonable" settlement. A small bite out of the enormous tax apple Joe owed.

The Harlem Globetrotters tried next. They played a benefit game for Joe's taxes. Another small bite out of the apple. Uncle Sam was not letting go, and he made everyone know it.

Rose tried. But she, like Marva, wanted a husband who was around, and Joe, well . . . ! They separated in the summer of 1957. The marriage was annulled the following year. It was shortly after this that Joe was introduced to Martha Malone Jefferson, the first black woman to be admitted to the bar in California. Joe flew to Los Angeles to meet her on the recommendation of a friend. He had talked to Martha over the telephone, liked what he heard. And when he met her in person he liked her even more.

Again the tax people showed up for a talk with Joe. He was asked, and agreed, to sign an agreement to pay $20,000 a year on the back taxes. Through refereeing the wrestling matches and his other holdings with the Louis-Rowe agency, Joe was making about $33,000 a year. Take from that the $12,000 tax he paid on his yearly income, the $20,000 he had agreed to pay back, and Louis was left with $1,000 to live on. Good old Uncle!

Martha Malone Jefferson now became the one ray of bright light in the darkness. She was smooth and cultured and nice, as well as being one hell of a woman lawyer. Joe felt better around her. There were no way out highs like he was used to, but no really low lows either. It was more of a steady thing with Martha around. Maybe that was what the ex-champion needed.

Joe asked Martha to marry him, and in a simple civil ceremony, Martha Malone Jefferson became the third Mrs. Joe Louis Barrow. Moreover, she became his lawyer in the tax fight with Uncle Sam, and finally, in 1960, got the tax people loose from Joe's back. Perhaps, indeed, Martha was just what Joe needed.

There were no crystal balls around for Joe then either, no way of knowing what was going to happen at the end of the new decade. So much had happened already that there didn't seem to be much of anything of any consequence that could happen now. Joe settled into his marriage, and it was good for a time. And Martha was more of a wife than the attorney she'd have to be when things got bad in May, 1970.

24

Beyond 1970: the champ had just punched toe-to-toe in a close bout with death and was struggling to regain his health and spirits. The *National Enquirer* had made an appeal to readers, telling how much Joe needed a lift. 20,500 responded with get-well cards and letters. The Paradise Valley branch post office in Las Vegas began delivering 1,200 pieces of mail to the Louis home each day.

"Just knowing that people care for him so much has given Joe a real mental lift!" declared his wife, Martha.

Joe underwent heart surgery in 1977 and suffered a stroke soon after. The toll it took on him was terrible, damaging his legs with near paralysis and badly affecting his speech. "The legs that once stalked opponents in the ring and carried him through twelve unforgettable years as heavyweight champion were rendered limp and useless,'' wrote the *Enquirer*.

Quoting his housekeeper, Pilar Aldana, they wrote, "It's really been a morale booster for Joe. I've been reading the cards and letters to him—but he's even been opening some of the mail himself. And a lot of it has brought a smile back to his face—something we haven't seen for a while. People wrote about the old times and how great he used to be. Many said that he was still the greatest, even greater than Muhammad Ali. Some wrote about how they remembered listening to his fights on the radio. And nearly everybody said they were praying for him to get well. A lot of schoolchildren have also been writing to him. They've been making their own get-well cards with little hearts and boxing gloves on them. It's beautiful. It really is!''

Martha, too, was grateful for the encouragement Joe received. "Joe's getting the strength back in his legs,'' the *Enquirer* quoted her saying. "He requires very little assistance to get in and out of his wheelchair or bed. In fact, on a couple of occasions, he's been able to get out of bed and into his wheelchair on his own. It's a major breakthrough.'' Martha said appreciatively, "On behalf of Joe, I would like to thank all those who took the time to write. Thank you—everyone—for remembering him and caring about him.''

Someone remembers, Joe Louis, make no mistake. Despite commitments and strokes, whatever—the Brown Bomber, Jolting Joe, the Detroit Mauler . . . whatever name he went by at whatever time, Joe Louis Barrow was one of the greatest world champions that ever entered the ring.

Thank God for memories that can never be taken away . . . not even for back taxes.

On October 7, 1977, Louis suffered a heart attack and a cerebral hemorrhage but returned to work at Caesar's in a wheelchair. Here he is shown with singer Frank Sinatra.

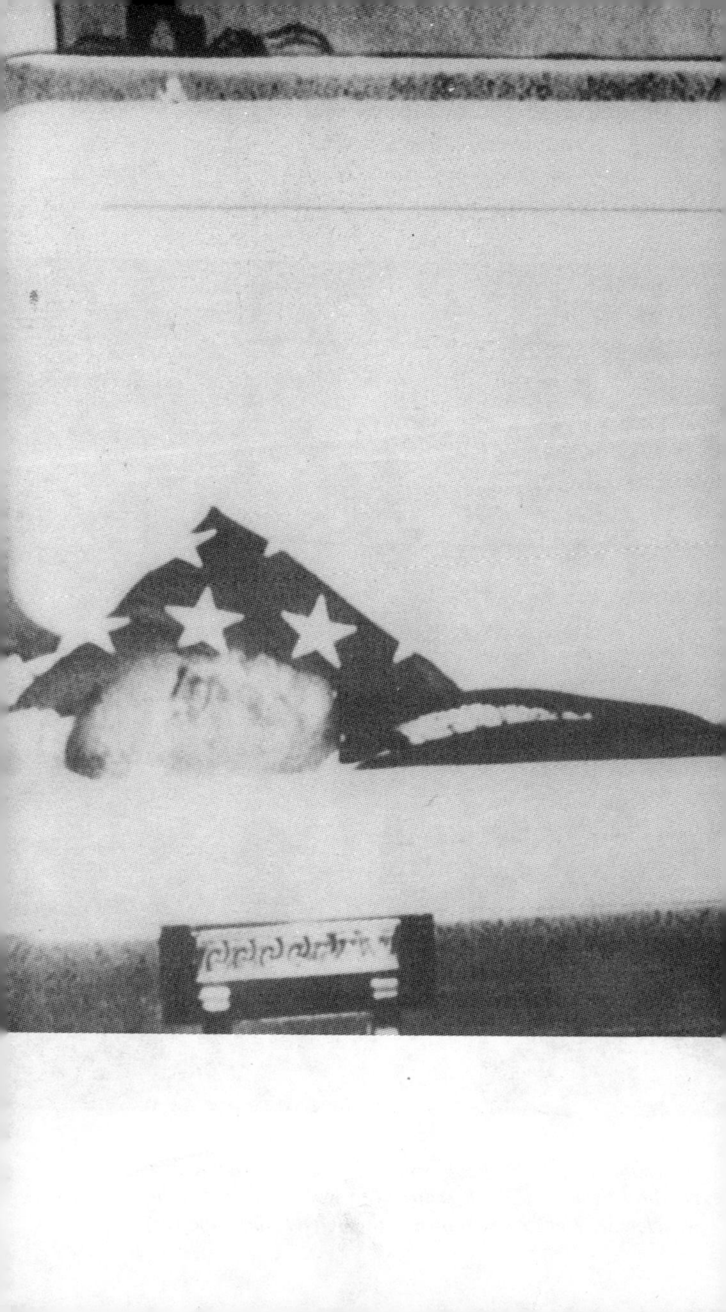

April 20, 1981: Martha Louis (a California lawyer) stands beside the coffin of her late husband at the Washington, D. C. services. He was interred in Arlington National Cemetery. He died of a heart attack eight days earlier in Las Vegas, having attended a boxing match the night before where he received a standing ovation.

RING RECORD OF JOE LOUIS

1934

DATE	OPPONENT	LOCATION	DECISION & ROUND
7/4	Jack Kracken	Chicago	Knockout 1
7/11	Willie Davis	Chicago	Knockout 3
7/29	Larry Udell	Chicago	Knockout 2
8/13	Jack Kranz	Chicago	Decision 6
8/27	Buck Everett	Chicago	Knockout 2
9/11	Alex Borchuk	Detroit	Knockout 2
9/24	Adolph Wiater	Chicago	Knockout 10
10/24	Art Sykes	Chicago	Knockout 8
10/30	Jack O'Dowd	Chicago	Knockout 2
11/14	Stanley Poreda	Chicago	Knockout 1
11/30	Charley Massera	Chicago	Knockout 3
12/14	Lee Ramage	Chicago	Knockout 3

1935

DATE	OPPONENT	LOCATION	DECISION & ROUND
1/4	Patsy Perroni	Detroit	Decision 10
1/11	Hans Birkie	Pittsburgh	Knockout 10
2/21	Lee Ramage	Los Angeles	Knockout 2
3/8	Donald "Reds" Barry	San Francisco	Knockout 3
3/28	Natie Brown	Detroit	Decision 10
4/12	Roy Lazer	Chicago	Knockout 3
4/22	Biff Benton	Dayton	Knockout 2
4/27	Roscoe Toles	Flint	Knockout 6

5/3	Willie Davis	Peoria	Knockout	2
5/7	Gene Stanton	Kalamazoo	Knockout	3
6/25	Primo Carnera	New York	Knockout	6
8/7	King Levinsky	Chicago	Knockout	1
9/24	Max Baer	New York	Knockout	4
12/13	Paolino Uzcudun	New York	Knockout	4

1936

1/17	Charley Retzlaff	Chicago	Knockout	1
6/19	Max Schmeling	New York	Knockout	12
8/17	Jack Sharkey	New York	Knockout	3
9/22	Al Ettore	Philadelphia	Knockout	5
10/9	Jorge Brescia	New York	Knockout	3
10/14	Willie Davis	South Bend	Exh. KO	3
10/14	K.O. Brown	South Bend	Exh. KO	2
11/20	Paul Williams	New Orleans	Exh. KO	3
11/20	Tom Jones	New Orleans	Exh. KO	3
12/14	Eddie Simms	Cleveland	Knockout	1

1937

1/11	Steve Ketchel	Buffalo	Knockout	2
1/27	Bob Pastor	New York	Decision	10
*2/17	Natie Brown	Kansas City	Knockout	4
*6/22	James J. Braddock	Chicago	Knockout	8

(Won the Heavyweight Campionship of the World)

*8/30	Tommy Farr	New York	Decision	15

* Denotes Title Fight

1938

*2/22	Nathan Mann	New York	Knockout	3
*4/1	Harry Thomas	Chicago	Knockout	5
*6/22	Max Schmeling	New York	Knockout	1

1939

*1/25	John Henry Lewis	New York	Knockout	1
*4/17	Jack Roper	Los Angeles	Knockout	1
*6/28	Tony Galento	New York	Knockout	4
*9/20	Bob Pastore	Detroit	Knockout	11

1940

*2/9	Arturo Godoy	New York	Decision	15
*3/29	Johnny Paycheck	New York	Knockout	2
*6/20	Arturo Godoy	New York	Knockout	8
*12/16	Al McCoy	Boston	Knockout	6

1941

*1/31	Red Burman	New York	Knockout	5
*2/17	Gus Dorazo	Philadelphia	Knockout	2
*3/21	Abe Simon	Detroit	Knockout	13
*4/8	Tony Musto	St. Louis	Knockout	9
*5/23	Buddy Baer	Washington, D.C.	Disq.	7
*6/18	Billy Conn	New York	Knockout	13
7/11	Jim Robinson	Minneapolis	Exh. KO	1
*9/29	Lou Nova	New York	Knockout	6

| 11/25 | George Giambastiani | Los Angeles | Exh. KO | 4 |

1942

*1/9	Buddy Baer	New York	Knockout	1
*3/27	Abe Simon	New York	Knockout	6
6/5	George Nicholson	Fort Hamilton	Exh.	3

1944
EXHIBITIONS

11/3	Johnny Demson	Detroit	Knockout	2
11/6	Charley Crump	Baltimore	Decision	3
11/9	Dee Amos	Hartford	Decision	3
11/13	Jimmy Bell	Washington, D.C.	Decision	3
11/14	Johnny Davis	Buffalo	Knockout	1
11/15	Dee Amos	Elizabeth	Decision	3
11/17	Dee Amos	Camden	Decision	3
11/24	Dan Merritt	Chicago	Decision	3

1945
EXHIBITIONS

11/15	Sugar Lip Anderson	San Francisco	Exh.	2
11/15	Big Boy Brown	Sacramento	Exh.	2
11/29	Bobby Lee	Sacramento	Exh.	2
11/29	Big Boy Brown	Sacramento	Exh.	2
12/10	Bob Frazier	Victoria	Exh.	3

12/11	Dave Johnson	Portland	Exh.	2
12/12	Big Boy Brown	Eugene	Exh.	3
12/13	Big Boy Brown	Vancouver	Exh.	3

1946

*6/19	Billy Conn	New York	Knockout	8
*9/18	Tami Mauriello	New York	Knockout	1
11/11	Cleo Everett	Honolulu	Exh.	4
11/11	Wayne Powell	Honolulu	Exh.	2
11/25	Perk Daniels	Mexicali	Exh.	4

1947

2/7	Arturo Godoy	Mexico City	Exh.	10
2/10	Art Ramsey	San Salvador	Exh.	3
2/10	Walter Haefer	San Salvador	Exh.	3
2/12	Art Ramsey	Panama City	Exh.	3
2/12	Walter Haefer	Panama City	Exh.	3
2/19	Arturo Godoy	Santiago	Exh.	6
2/27	Art Ramsey	Medellin	Exh.	2
2/27	Walter Haefer	Medellin	Exh.	2
3/10	Walter Haefer	Havana	Exh.	2
3/10	Art Ramsey	Havana	Exh.	2
6/10	Rusty Payne	San Diego	Exh.	2
6/10	Dick Underwood	San Diego	Exh.	2
6/13	Tiger Jack Fox	Spokane	Exh.	4
6/23	Harry Wills	Los Angeles	Exh.	4

Date	Opponent	Location	Result	Rounds
*12/5	Jersey Joe Walcott	New York	Decision	15

1948

Date	Opponent	Location	Result	Rounds
1/29	Bob Foxworth	Chicago	Exh.	4
*5/25	Jersey Joe Walcott	New York	Knockout	11
9/30	Pat Comiskey	Washington, D.C.	Exh.	6
10/28	Bob Garner	Atlanta	Exh.	3
10/28	Merritt Wynn	Atlanta	Exh.	3
10/29	Bob Garner	Norfolk	Exh.	4
10/31	Bob Garner	New Orleans	Exh.	4
11/1	Bob Garner	New Orleans	Exh.	3
11/3	Bob Garner	Nashville	Exh.	4
11/8	Johnny Shkor	Boston	Exh.	4
11/9	Bernie Reynolds	New Haven	Exh.	4
11/17	Jimmy Bivins	Cleveland	Exh.	6
11/19	Vern Mitchell	Detroit	Exh.	6
11/23	Kid Riviera	St. Louis	Exh.	6
11/24	Ray Augustus	Oklahoma City	Exh. KO	2
11/25	Curt Kennedy	Kansas City	Exh.	4
11/29	Billy Smith	Cincinnati	Exh.	4
12/10	Billy Conn	Chicago	Exh.	6
12/14	Arturo Godoy	Philadelphia	Exh.	6
12/16	Pat Comiskey	Paterson	Exh.	6
12/20	Willie James	Lewiston	Exh.	4

1949

Date	Opponent	Location	Result	
1/10	Sterling Ingram	Omaha	Exh.	4
1/11	Orlando Ott	Topeka	Exh.	4
1/12	Hubert Hood	Wichita	Exh.	4
1/17	Art Swiden	Toledo	Exh.	4
1/18	Dick Hagen	Moline, Illinois	Exh.	4
1/19	Orlando Ott	Rochester	Exh.	4
1/25	Elmer Ray	Miami	Exh.	6
1/27	George Fitch	Palm Beach	Exh.	4
1/28	Nino Valdez	Tampa	Exh.	4
1/31	Dixie Lee Oliver	Orlando	Exh. KO	4
2/1	Elmer Ray	Jacksonville	Exh.	4
2/4	Bill Graves	Daytona Beach	Exh. KO	3
2/4	George Fitch	Savannah	Exh.	4
2/23	Edgar Edward	Kingston, Jamaica	Exh.	3
3/1	(Louis announces his retirement as undefeated World Heavyweight Champion.)			
3/1	Ed Crawley	Nassau	Exh.	4
3/4	Omelio Agramonte	Havana	Exh.	4
3/5	Omelio Agramonte	Oriente	Exh.	4
3/16	Elmer Ray	Houston	Exh. KO	4
3/18	Tex Boddie	Dallas	Exh.	4
3/22	Hubert Hood	St. Paul	Exh.	6
3/22	Abel Cestac	Washington, D.C.	Exh.	4
10/10	Curtiss Sheppard	Baltimore	Exh.	4
10/24	Bill Weinberg	Providence	Exh.	4

Date	Opponent	Location	Result	Rounds
10/25	Joe Domonic	Hartford	Exh.	4
10/31	Bill Gilliam	Atlantic City	Exh.	4
11/14	Johnny Shkor	Boston	Exh. No Decision	10
11/22	Joe Chesul	Newark	Exh. No Decision	10
11/28	Johnny Flynn	Kansas City	Exh. No Decision	10
12/7	Pat Valentino	Chicago	Exh. KO	8
12/14	Roscoe Toles	Detroit	Exh.	5
12/14	Johnny Flynn	Detroit	Exh.	5
12/19	Al Hoosman	Oakland	Exh. KO	5
12/21	Jay Lambert	Salt Lake City	Exh.	5
12/21	Rex Layne	Salt Lake City	Exh.	5

1950

Date	Opponent	Location	Result	Rounds
1/6	Willie Bean	Hollywood	Exh.	6
1/10	Jack Flood	Seattle	Exh.	6
1/12	Clarence Henry	Wilmington	Exh.	4
1/13	Al Spaulding	San Diego	Exh.	4
1/20	Andy Walker	Stockton	Exh.	4
1/24	Rex Layne	Salt Lake City	Exh.	4
2/1	Gene Jones	Miami	Exh.	8
2/7	Nino Valdez	St. Petersberg	Exh.	4
2/8	Candy McDaniels	Orlando	Exh.	5
2/14	Johnny Haynes	Tampa	Exh.	4
2/21	Sid Peaks	Jacksonville	Exh.	6
2/23	Dan Bolston	Macon	Exh.	1
2/23	Leo Jackson	Macon	Exh.	3

Date	Opponent	Location	Result	
2/27	Willie Johnson	Albany, Georgia	Exh.	4
2/28	Dan Bolston	Columbus, Georgia	Exh.	4
3/3	Leo Johnson	Waycross, Georgia	Exh.	4
3/18	Kid Carr	Lubbock	Exh.	4
3/20	Sterling Ingram	Odessa	Exh.	4
3/22	Joe Stantell	El Paso	Exh.	4
3/22	John McFalls	El Paso	Exh.	4
3/24	Henry Hall	Austin	Exh.	4
3/25	J.K. Homer	Waco	Exh.	4
4/22	Walter Haefer	Rio de Janeiro	Exh. KO	2
*9/27	Ezzard Charles	New York	Loss	15
11/29	Cesar Brion	New York	Decision	10

1951

Date	Opponent	Location	Result	
1/3	Freddie Beshore	Detroit	Knockout	4
2/7	Omelio Agramonte	Miami	Decision	10
2/23	Andy Walker	San Francisco	Knockout	10
5/2	Omelio Agramonte	Detroit	Decision	10
6/15	Lee Savold	New York	Knockout	6
8/1	Cesar Brion	San Francisco	Decision	10
8/15	Jimmy Bivins	Baltimore	Decision	10
10/26	Rocky Marciano	New York	Loss	8
11/18	U.S. Serviceman	Tokyo	Knockout	4
11/18	U.S. Serviceman	Tokyo	Knockout	4

11/18	U.S. Serviceman	Tokyo	Exh.	3
11/18	Cpl. Buford J. DeCordova	Tokyo	Exh.	4
11/18	Cpl. Buford J. DeCordova	Tokyo	Exh.	4
12/14	Sgt. Lindy Brooks	Sanda	Exh.	3
12/14	Chang Pulu	Taipei	Knockout	1
12/14	Sgt. Seth E. Woodbury	Taipei	Exh.	2
12/14	D.H. Cantrell (U.S. Navy)	Taipei	Exh.	2
12/14	Cpl. Buford J. DeCordova	Taipei	Exh.	3
12/16	Cpl. Buford J. DeCordova	Taipei	Exh.	3

INDEX

133rd Street, 96
140th Street, 96
"a hit," 43
Adirondacks, 28-29
Africa, 98, 169
Agramonte, Omelio, 190
Alabama Assassin, 89
Aldana, Pilar, 198
Alexander the Great, 143
Ali, Muhammad, *see*
  Muhammad Ali
America(ns), 15, 28-30, 98,
  105, 142-143, 151,
  153-154, 160, 166, 169,
  171, 175
American Way, The, 11
Amsterdam News, 96
Anchors Aweigh, 95
Andrews, Irving P., 79
Arcadia Gardens, 71, 82
Argentina, 18
Armed Forces, 167
Armstrong, Henry, 194
Aryan Hope, 10, 13, 28, 33
Army Relief Fund, 159-160,
  167
Atlantic Ocean, 26, 29, 34,
  105
Bacon Casino, 55
Baer, Buddy, 144, 151-153
Baer, Max, 24, 45, 94, 98,
  101, 103-105, 111-112,
  115, 144-146, 149-150,
  154
Baksi, Joe, 177
Barnett, Charlie, 140
Barrow, Emmarell, 45, 47,
  85

Barrow, Joe Louis Jr., 177
Barrow, Lily Reese, 37, 39,
  48, 69
Barrow, Munrow, 37, 39
Barrow, Vunice, 14, 17, 40,
  44, 142, 194
Barry, Donald "Reds,"
  89-90
Basie,Count, *see* Count Basie
Bauer, Joe, 58-59
Bedford Hills, New York,
  132
Bennett, Robert C., 78,
  155-157
Benton, Biff, 93
Berlin, Germany, 116
Bermuda, 153
Beshore, Freddie, 190
Bier, Joseph, 97
Bimstein, Whitey, 118
Birkie, Hans, 88, 116
Black, Julian, 58, 61-63,
  65-67, 69-70, 81, 83,
  91-93, 101, 112, 116-118,
  122, 136, 141, 145, 154,
  162
Black America, 122
Black Power, 59
Blackburn, "Chappie," 12,
  14, 16-17, 19, 22-23, 25,
  61-67, 70-72, 82, 84,
  87-88, 91, 94, 97, 99-101,
  103, 105, 112, 114,
  116-119, 122, 124-126,
  138, 140-141, 147-148,
  152-153, 160-162,
  169-170, 173-178, 180
Boll Weevil, 41

Borchuk, Alex, 69, 71
Boston, Massachusetts, 183
Bottoms, Bill, 62, 94, 98
Braddock, James, 20-25, 98,
    101, 103, 116, 118, 123,
    146
"breakfast of champions," 9
Brescia, Jorge, 18
Brewster's East Side
    Gymnasium, 46, 53
Bridges, Clayton, 55
Briggs Stadium, 139
British Empire, 191
Brofman, David, 77-78
Bronson School, 44
Brooklyn Dodgers, 172
Brooks, Patrick, 39-42,
    48-49, 52-53, 85
Brooks, Patrick, Jr., 40
Brown, Bingo, 69-70
Brown Bomber, book, 157
Brown, Natie, 20, 90-91
Buckalew Mountain, 38,
    40-42
Buick, automobile, 111-112,
    142
Bum of the Month Club,
    143-146, 148
Burman, Red, 144
Calloway, Cab, 96, 162
Camp Hill, 40
Camp Upton, New York, 154
Campanella, Roy, 194
Canada, 69
Carnera, Primo, 16, 90-94,
    97-101, 104-105, 114-115,
    150
Canzoneri, Tony, 123
Capone, Al, 43
Catherine Street Gang, 48

Catherine Theater, 45
Ceasar's Palace, 127
Central America, 177
Central Park, 94
Chan, Charley, 122
Charles, Ezzard, 184, 186,
    188-191
Charles, Ray, 44
Chavallo, George, 70
Chicago, Illinois, 21, 23, 25,
    35, 43, 55, 57-59, 61-63,
    65-66, 71, 81-85, 88, 93,
    101, 118, 126, 136, 181,
    184
Chicago Black Hawks, 184
Chicago Defender, 84, 96
Chicago Stadium, 82-83,
    183-185
Chicano(s), 43
Christmas Day, 85, 107-108,
    112, 183, 194
Christmas Eve, 107
"Cinderella Man," 24
Civil Rights Movement, 83
Clay, Cassius, *see also*
    Muhammad Ali, 18, 27
Cleveland, Ohio, 19, 88, 183
Coles, Truman, 79
Colorado General Hospital,
    76
Colorado Psychiatric
    Hospital, 77-79, 108
Comiskey Park, 21, 23-24
Conn, Billy, 146-150,
    167-171, 173-175, 178,
    182-183
"cosmic punch," 149
Cotton Club, 96-97, 111, 141
Count Basie, 194
coup de grace, 57, 194

Cowans, Russell, 112-113
crackers, 40
Cream, Arnold, 177
Crosby, Bing, 139
Cuba, 139, 185
Cusseta, Alabama, 37-40,
    42-43
Dallas, Ruby, 141
Dark Destroyer, 89
Davis, Willie, 68, 93
Dayton, Helen, 155-156
Dayton, Ohio, 93
Dempsey, Jack, 48, 91, 174,
    194-195
Denver, Colorado, 76, 79
Denver County, 78
Denver *Post*, 78
Denver Sheriff's Department,
    75
der Fuerher, 20
Detroit, Michigan, 14-15, 20,
    25, 35, 41-43, 45-47, 52,
    54, 56, 58, 60, 70-71, 78,
    85, 88, 90, 93-94, 125,
    130-132, 136, 139, 144,
    155, 169, 183, 190
Detroit Athletic Club, 55
Detroit Chronicle, 113
Detroit Destroyer, 89
Detroit Free Press, 44, 69
Detroit Mauler, 198
Detroit Police, 70
Detroit Red Wings, 184
Detroit River, 43
Donovan, Arthur, 13, 19,
    31-32, 118, 136, 138, 146,
    150, 175
Dorazio, Gus, 144
Doughtery, Rowan, 96
Duffield School, 44, 46

Dundee, Johnny, 123
Duquesne Garden, 88
Durante, Jimmy, 125
East Coast, 91
Easter Sunday, 93
Eastern Vegetable and
    Produce Market, 44
Edgar, Eddie, 69
Edward J. Neil Trophy, 151
Eggberg, Marion, 96, 110
Eisenhower, Dwight D., 194
Eleventh Street Police
    Station, 57
Ellington, Duke, 96
Ellis, Atler, 46, 48, 51-52,
    54
Ellison, James, 78
Europe, 10, 98, 105, 169,
    175
Empire State Building, 176
Ethiopia, 98, 100
Ettore, Al, 18
Evans, Stanley, 56, 58
Everett, Buck, 69
Fake, Guy L., 22
Far East, 191
Farnsworth, Bill, 124
Flecher, Dusty, 95
Fleisher, Nat, 90, 123
Forbes, Frank, 179
Ford Field, 58
Ford Motor Company, 42, 53
Forest Athletic Club, 54
Fort Hamilton, New York,
    165
Fort Riley, Kansas, 165-166
Foxworth, Bob, 181-182
Franklin, Bennie, 45
Frazier, Joe, 131
Frog Club, 91

Fullam, Frank, 182
Galento, "Two-Ton" Tony, 136-138
Garvey, Marcus, 98, 153
Gary, Indiana, 57
Germany, 10, 13, 21, 27-33, 117, 125, 161
Gibson, Truman, 184
Gibson, Truman Jr., 167
Godoy, Arturo, 140-141, 177
Goebbels, Paul Joseph, 20-21, 27
Golden, Leo, 121
Golden Gloves, 46-47, 55, 57-58, 65
Goldstein, Ruby, 179, 191
Goliath, 13, 99
Grand Hotel, 84
Great Depression, The, 43-45, 56, 142
Green Bay, Wisconsin, 71
Greenlee, Gus, 116
Guinyard, Freddie, 44-45, 52, 65, 126, 156-157, 194
Hamas, Steve, 116
Hamburg, Germany, 116
Harlem, New York, 14, 17, 34, 94-95, 105, 122, 126, 129-130, 172, 181
Harlem Globetrotters, 195
Harlem Opera House, 95
Harris, Edna Mae, 122
Hearst, William Randolph, 90
Hearst Milk Fund, 90, 98
Heavyweight Crown, 148
Helmer, Arno, 29, 31, 33
Henie, Sonja, 122
Hereford Cows, 137
Hillcrest Country Club, 151
Hippodrome, The, 18, 125

Hitchcock, Alfred, 14
Hitler, Adolf, 10-12, 20, 30, 34, 166, 175
Hoboken, New Jersey, 81
Holly, Edna Mae, 97
Hollywood, California, 115, 121-122
Honolulu, Hawaii, 177
Hopkins, Claude, 96
Horne, Lena, 97, 111, 140
Hotel Theresa, 14, 17
Howard University, 142
Hudson's Department Store, 45
IBC, 189
Igoe, Hype, 96
Impellitteri, Vincent, 190
International League, 172
Italy, 169
Jacobs, Mike, 16, 20-21, 30, 34-35, 90-92, 94, 96, 101, 103, 112, 118, 125, 143, 151, 153, 167, 171, 174, 177, 183, 185
Japan(ese), 10, 150, 152-153
Jefferson, Martha Malone, as Mrs. Joe Louis Barrow, 196, 198
Jeffries, Jim, 185
Jim Crow Laws, 169
Joe Louis Punch, 187
Joe Louis: My Life, 38
Johnson, Jack, 48, 64, 72, 91, 97, 110, 112-115, 139, 143
Johnson, Marie, 131-132, 155
Johnston, James, 19, 87
Jolting Joe, 198
Jones, Buck, 45
Jones, Ted, 150

Journal American, 96
Jumbo, 125
Kalamazoo, Michigan, 93
Kansas City, Kansas, 20, 168
Kenosha, Wisconsin, 22
Kid Chocolate, 48
Kracken, Jack, 65-66, 68
Ku Klux Klan, 40
Lafayette, Alabama, 38
Lafayetteville, New York, 28
Lake Michigan, 22
Lakewood, New Jersey, 16
Las Vegas, Nevada, 127-128,
  197
Lazer, Roy, 93
Lee, Cowboy Rocky, 195
Legion Of Merit Medal, 171
Lehman, Herbert, 29
Lenny, Harry, 22
Lenox Avenue, 96
Lesnevich, Gus, 186
Levinsky, Harry "Kingfish,"
  101, 103, 114
Lewis, John Henry, 116,
  135-136
Lincoln Cemetary, 162
Lockhart, Al, 187
London, England, 169
Long Island City, New York,
  20, 154
Long's Drugstore, 56
Los Angeles, California, 51,
  83, 88, 107-108, 128, 137,
  151, 177, 188, 195
Loughran, Tommy, 123
Louis, "Punchie," 77, 177
Louis, Jacqueline, 77, 108,
  169
Louis, Joe, 9-10, 12-15,
  17-25, 27-28, 30, 32-35,
  38, 41-47, 49, 52-56,
  58-63, 66-69, 71-73,
  75-79, 81, 83-85, 87-90,
  92- 97, 100-101, 103-106,
  109-110, 112-114,
  116-117, 119, 121-133,
  135-145, 147-163, 165,
  167-174, 177-183, 185-198
birth of, 37
as the Brown Bomber, 9, 11,
  13-14, 17-22, 24-25,
  27-28, 31, 34, 42, 48,
  51-52, 71, 79, 89, 90-93,
  95, 98, 100, 104-105,
  110-112, 118, 133,
  137-138, 145-146, 161,
  174, 176, 180, 182,
  189-191, 193, 198
Louis, Martha, 76-77,
  107-110, 127-133, 157
Louis, Marva, 14-15, 17, 34,
  75-76, 103, 105, 115-116,
  119, 122-123, 135-137,
  139-140, 142, 144-146,
  168-170, 172-173, 175,
  177, 183, 187-188,
  194-195
Louis, Rose Morgan, 194-195
Louis XV, as a style of
  decor, 77, 79
Louis-Rowe Agency, 194,
  196
MacDonald, John H., 76-78
MacDonald's Choice, 139
Machon, Max, 28, 33
Madden, Owney, 97
Madison Avenue, 43
Madison Square Garden,
  19-20, 22, 81, 87-88, 90,
  92, 114, 117, 131,

151-152, 159, 178, 184, 189, 191
Mafia, 155
Manhattan, 132
Marciano, Rocky, 191
Marek, Max, 55
Marigold Gardens, 68
Massera, Charley, 44, 82-83
Mathis, Buster, 131
Mauriello, Tami, 176
Maynard, Ken, 45
Mayo Clinic, 136
McCoy, Al
McKinney, Thurston, 46-49, 52, 54
McNichols, Stephen L.R., 76-77
Memo Club, 96
Mendel, Harry, 176
Mexicali, Mexico, 177
Miami, Florida, 128, 183
Michigan Mauler, 89
Michigan State Boxing Commission, 69
Miler, Johnny, 51-53
Miles, Marshall, 174-175, 190
Minneapolis, Minnesota, 149
Mitchell, Benny, 48, 60, 70, 85, 88
Mix, Tom, 45
Monaco Parkway, 78
Monongahela, Pennsylvania, 82
Monroe, Al, 84, 96
Monroe, Marty, 179
Montreal Royals, 172
Morley, Mantan, 122
Muhammad Ali, 198
Murphy, Frank, 34

Muskogee, Oklahoma, 85
Mussolini, Benito, 98, 100, 105
Musto, Tony, 144
N.B.A., 185
Napanoch, New York, 125
National Enquirer, 197-198
Naval Amory, 52, 69
Navy Relief Fund, 151-152
Navy Relief Society, 159
Nazi Bund, 31
Nazis, 10, 12-13, 28, 35
Nazism, 10, 20, 26-27, 29, 33-34, 89, 110, 153, 161
Negro Elks, 9
Negro National League, 116
Negroes, 42, 64, 115, 122
Nelson, Carl, 23, 162
Nelson, Donald, 160
New Orleans, Lousiana, 19
New York Athletic Commission, 180
New York Boxing Commission, 185
New York City, New York, 14, 20-21, 33, 72, 87-88, 90, 94, 96, 99, 101, 104, 107-109, 119, 122, 128-129, 140-141, 144, 146, 150-151, 153, 180, 185, 192
New York *Daily News*, 119
New York Sheraton, 110
New York State Athletic Commission, 22, 177
New York State Office Building, 99
Newark, New Jersey, 22
Nicholson, George, 28, 165
Nixon, Richard M., 78

Norfolk, Nebraska, 195
Norris, Jim, 184, 189, 191
Norway, 122
Notre Dame, 55
Nova, Lou, 149-150
Oakland, California, 128
Oklahoma City, Oklahoma, 183
Olin, Bob, 116
Olympic Arena, 88
Olympic Games, 51
Orange, New Jersey, 137
Pacific Ocean, 105
Park Sheraton, 108, 128-129, 155
Pastor, Bob, 19-20, 139-140, 179
Patterson, Robert, 160
Paycheck, Johnny, 150
Pearl Harbor, 151-152
Peoria, Illinois, 93
Perroni, Patsy, 88
"phantom fight," 22
Philadelphia, Pennsylvania, 18, 114, 144
Philippines, 175
Pilgrim Baptist Church, 162
Pittsburg, Pennsylvania, 116
Pittsburg Courier, 96, 173
Polo Grounds, New York, 149
Pompton Lakes, New Jersey, 16-17, 29, 32, 97-98, 103-104, 112, 117, 173
Poreda, Stanley, 81-82
Purple Gang, 43
Ramage, Lee, 83-84, 88-89, 116, 137
Red Rooster, 129-130
Reddish, Willie, 28

Reeves, George, 195
Republican Party, 142
Retzlaff, Charley, 118-119, 121
Ring Magazine, 90, 123, 192
Risko, Johnny, 71
River Rouge, 53
Robert Ripley's Flea Circus, 115
Robinson, Bill "Bojangles," 96, 116, 162
Robinson, Donald, 165-167
Robinson, Jackie, 165-167
Robinson, Jim, 149
Robinson, Sugar Ray, 97, 168-169, 190
Rocky Mountain News, 78
Roosevelt, Franklin D., 9-10, 28, 30, 35, 142-143, 160
Rowe, Billy, 96, 172-173, 175, 185
Roxborough(s), The, 56-60, 62, 65-66, 69-70, 72, 81-82, 87-88, 90-93, 98, 101, 103, 112, 114-118, 122, 124, 136, 141-142, 145-146, 169-170, 172, 175
Ruggerillo, Salvatore, 124
Ruth, Babe, 31
Saint Nicholas Avenue, 34
San Diego, California, 177
San Francisco, California, 89, 186
Savold, Lee, 191
"scalping," 30
Schmeling, Max, 10-15, 18-21, 24, 26-34, 105, 110, 117-119, 123-126, 135, 150, 153

Seamon, Mannie, 173-174,
  190
Sepia Socker, 89
Seventh Avenue, 94, 96
Shanburg, Elliott, 121
Sharkey, Jack, 16-18, 20, 94
Sheley, Peter, 39
Siberia, 12
Simms, Eddie, 19
Simon, Abe, 144, 159-160
Sinai Baptist Church, 38
Slayton, George, 55-56
Smith, Harry, 89
"somezing," 13
South Bend, Indiana, 18
South Side, Chicago, 26, 65
South Side, Miami, 183
Spaulding, Albert, 188
Sperber, Harry, 29
Spokane, Washington, 177
Spring Hill, New Jersey,
  139, 142, 145
St. Albans, Long Island, 194
St. Louis, Missouri, 116,
  144, 183
St. Valentine's Day, 128
Stanton, Gene, 93
Staten Island Ferry, 176
Stevensville, Michigan, 22
Steubenville, Ohio, 132
Strauss, Sol, 22
Sullivan, Ed, 119
Swastika, 10
Sullivan, John L., 146
Sykes, Art, 72, 81
Tabani, Ray, 194
Tandberg, Ollie, 177
Temple, Shirley, 116
Thanksgiving Day, 151
The North, 42

The Organization, 43
The South, 40
The Spirit of Youth, 121
The Syndicate, 43
Thomas, Tommy, 25, 55
Third Reich, 31
This Is The Army, 168
Toles, Roscoe, 93
Trotter, Marva, 84-85, 88,
  94
Trujillo, Mose, 78
Turner, Lana, 141
Twentieth Century Sporting
  Club, 20, 90, 284
U.S. Army, 153, 159,
  161-162, 165-166,
  168-169, 172
U.S. Navy, 165
U.S. Supreme Court, 83
UCLA, 166
Udell, Larry, 68
Uncle Sam, 172, 175, 182,
  186-187, 189, 195-196
United States, 10-11, 31, 98,
  153, 184
United States Government,
  188
United States Negro Horse
  Show, 139
University of Chicago, 84
Urban League, 56
Utica Riding Club, 139
Uzcudun, Paolino, 12-13,
  116-118
Valentino, Pat, 186
Vaterland, 20
Virginia Dare, 137
Vogue School of Design, 84
Walcott, Jersey Joe, 177-179,
  181-182, 184

Walker, Carl, 76, 78
War Department, 167-168
Washington, D.C., 9, 78,
    142, 168, 185
Washington, Chester, 96
Washington Park, 62, 64
Welfare Relief Program, 142
Wells, Dickie, 141
Western Europe, 27
Western World, 28
White House, 9, 78
Wiater, Adolph, 71
Willard, Jess, 139
Williams, Holman, 48-49,
    51-52, 54-55, 83
Willkie, Wendell, 142-143
Wilson, Freddie, 155-156
Wirtz, Arthur, 184
Woodard, Isaac, 175
World Publishing Company,
    157
World Series, 31
World War II, 27
Yankee Stadium, 11-12, 14,
    16-17, 94, 99, 104, 118,
    138, 141, 149, 171, 176,
    181, 189
Yoga, 149
Young Negro Progressive
    Association, 56
Youngheim, John, 195

TO KILL A BLACK MAN

By Louis E. Lomax

A compelling dual biography of the two men who changed America's way of thinking—Malcolm X and Martin Luther King, Jr.

Louis E. Lomax was a close friend to both Malcolm X and Dr. Martin Luther King, Jr. In this dual biography, he includes much that Malcolm X did not tell in his autobiography and dissects Malcolm's famous letters. Lomax writes with the sympathy and understanding of a friend but he is also quick to point out the shortcomings of both Dr. King and Malcolm X—and what he believed was the reasons for their failure to achieve their goals and to obtain the full support of all their people. And he does not hesitate in pointing a finger at those he believes to be responsible for the deaths of his friends. "A valuable addition to the available information on the murders of Martin Luther King, Jr. and Malcolm X," says the *Litterair Passport*. Louis Lomax gained national prominence with such books as *The Black Revolt, When The Word Is Given,* and *To Kill A Black Man.* At the time of his death in an automobile accident he was a professor at Hofstra University.

MELROSE SQUARE
BLACK AMERICAN SERIES

Melrose Square proudly announces a new series of Black American biographies. Each volume is profusely illustrated, meticulously researched, widely acclaimed. The first four titles are now available. Quality paperback format: $3.95 each.

PAUL ROBESON: ATHLETE, ACTOR, SINGER, ACTIVIST. Written by Scott Ehrlich, this is the story of the gifted man who went from All-American football player at Rutgers (where he graduated first in his class) to win worldwide respect as a performer.

ELLA FITZGERALD: FIRST LADY OF AMERICAN SONG. Written by Bud Kliment, this beautifully-told biography traces Ella's fascinating life from her birth in Virginia to her White House—and international—acclaim as America's "First Lady of Song."

NAT TURNER: PROPHET AND SLAVE LEADER. Written by Terry Bisson. Fiery preacher, militant leader—and prophet—Nat Turner organized a slave uprising that struck a defiant blow against slavery in the United States thirty years before the Civil War.

JACKIE ROBINSON: FIRST BLACK IN PROFESSIONAL BASEBALL. Written by Richard Scott. The story of the man who was good enough, professional enough and, most of all, man enough to be selected to break the "color barrier" in professional baseball.